Making Love

How Faith Fuels Our Practice of Love

Mark Spencer

Acknowledgements

I am a very rich man. The family, friendships, and relationships I've been granted puts me in a ridiculously blessed category. This book is proof of that. There are thousands of people's fingerprints on it. All the life stories people have so graciously invited me into. The churches where I attended and served: New Covenant, River of Life, City Hill, Vine, Harvest, Faith Covenant and Bridgewood have all taught me about love. The editors: Sharon, Laura, Nancy and Rebecca have kindly expressed their corrections with love and grace. Thank you! My teachers and mentors at Bethel Seminary marked my life with wisdom and love. My sisters and brother (Melanie, Lisa, Matt, and Mara) have offered a steady stream of love and support. Georgi, my mother, has been a powerhouse of love. All five feet of her loving with the force of a tsunami. My mother-in-law Barb has been a tremendous encourager to me. Thanks moms! Although both of my dads have passed (Ray and Andy) they shaped and formed my heart for people. My sister and brother in law, Steve and Becky have prayed long and hard for me. Thank you! Maria, Joe, Beka, John, and Ben (my children) have lovingly endured their dad's questions and jokes. Their spouses, girlfriend and our grandchildren now share their heavy load! (Mirko and Livi, Kristin and Hannah and Lucy, Bryan and Colt, Mande and Hallie, Allie). Finally, and chiefly, thank you to my wife Betsy. You are "love to me" and have made clear the way for this writer to risk love.

Table of Contents

Preface

I am not sure why you picked up this book. The title may have amused you. Your marriage may be struggling. I don't know. What I do know are two foundational truths. First, everyone craves love. Secondly, the love we crave is made. It's learned. It's work. And love is the best thing you will ever make. You don't fall into it. You don't find it. You don't discover it. You make it. I know some will push back and say, "but Mark we really fell in love." Nope. You fell into a high level of attraction; not love. Attraction can encourage you to start the work of love, but it won't carry the enduring weight of carefully made love. Love's production stretches us, provokes us, matures us, and fulfills us. Love is the very stuff of life and it's made. No wonder the Creator of all things reminds us, "A new command I give you: Love one another. As I have loved you, so you must love one another." (John 13:34).

As you begin reading, I want to encourage you to focus on you. Think about what you know about love. Review what you've been taught. Consider what you're living out now. Note what you may need to learn. For example, places where you are hesitant or unsure in the practice of your love. Think about the people who can best support and mentor you. Think about you. You will get to the "us" soon enough. A good "us" is comprised of two healthy "me's" who are committed to making love.

I write to you as one who keeps learning to love. It is challenging but deeply rewarding. My life is full and so is my heart. Dig in reader and may Love guide your way. Grace and peace as you read.

Chapter 1: Why Is Love So Hard

Love stories:

      Dan was the product of a fragmented family; in fact, his family has been shattered. By his 17th birthday he had "known" seven different "fathers". He comes to see me because his concept of God as his "father" is "just not happening" as he puts it. He repeatedly runs into a place where he needs to risk sharing more of himself with a friend or lover and just can't. In the midst of panic, he flees the relationship like a man on fire. Will he ever be able to love?

      Lisa, on the other hand, has just one dad. One would think she would have a solid foundation for love to rest on; however, that is far from the truth. Struggling to hold back a torrent of tears, her body convulses as she recounts the years her dad molested her. Instead of care, she experienced rape. Instead of protection she regularly endured violation. Instead of love she was hounded by lust. Will she ever love freely?

      David thought he was being wise by carefully waiting for "the one" God would send him. He prayed daily. He avoided the dating scene. He hoped if he maintained purity, he would in turn find pure love. Instead he discovered on their honeymoon that his new bride had been raped, and the terror was living on inside of her. In his words, "our marriage was over by honeymoon's end...*neither one of us had realized our dreams."* Can David ever muster the courage to try to love again?

Brett and Cindy have been together for 29 years, but Cindy has had it with him. She reports he never asks her about her. She is tired of pursuing him. Even in this conversation he sits stoically as if he is waiting for his medical appointment. No emotion. No comment. No engagement. Then when we map out his family, the map screams, "won't anybody see me?" His childhood is one long story of never being noticed for anything. Can Brett ever learn to notice anyone if no one noticed him?

Paul is a sensitive good-natured boy. His ten-year-old brown eyes reveal both a perceptive mind and a spark for life. That spark is sometimes clouded by the heated battles between his parents. He routinely scans the landscape of his world searching for signs of another potential blowout between his mom and dad. The arguments are fairly predictable and constant, what is not constant is who will stay and who will go. Despite having two older siblings around him, none of kids know how to make much sense of their setting. They tiptoe around these conflicts hoping to preserve some sliver of peace. Love isn't modeled here. At times it is offered, but it quickly changes form like an ice cream cone in the hot August sun; here one minute and gone the next.

You may have your own story of love's challenges. I do. They propelled me down this path of asking, "Why is love so hard?" I heard my parents argue. I watched my sister's bicker. I encountered my own share of battles. I've seen it on the playgrounds, at workplaces, on sports teams, in families. Everywhere. Wherever we go, the challenge to love follows.

So, is there hope? Yes. In fact, if we can begin by understanding that we learn love, that helps. The common notion of "falling in love" sounds so easy-like falling into a warm pool of water. However, there is nothing easy about true love. It doesn't just happen, and you certainly don't "fall into it." You learn it, and you make it. Throughout all the seasons of our lives we will be learning and making love. This book is inspired by the people whom I have watched and walked with as they learned to make love. They are real people just like you and me. They aren't "lucky", but they are devoted. They are determined "makers" of love. As you apply yourself to learn, you too can be confident lovers.

QUESTIONS:
- What do you think about the idea of "making" love as stated in this chapter so far?
- As you begin this book are you hopeful about growing in your capacity to give and receive love?
- When you finish this book, what do you hope is different?

Our Wiring

Our deepest desire is to find our people and our place. We are always looking for them. We continually search our social landscape in the hopes of settling our place and people. You see it right from the beginning of the Bible. God creates Adam then God gives him a place- the garden. Afterwards God does some quality control and declares, "it is not good for man to be alone." So, God gives Adam his people-Eve. This pattern of people and place is all through the biblical story. Israel moves from slavery to a promised land, each tribe finding their place with their own people. The story of Ruth portrays our deep need for people and place in a young girl who although caring for her mother-in-law she herself has no one to care for her. But God helps Ruth find her people and place with Boaz. Jesus promises eternally to go and make a place for us so we can be with him. People and place. It is core to our humanity.

Given God built us this way, our souls unravel if we can't rest in our "place" or safely be with our "people". Loneliness, isolation, and rejection are hugely corrosive to our soul. When hurt in a relationship, alone and away might feel safe for a moment, but eventually our wiring spurs us unto a new search for our people and place.

Think about how many of us feel when we walk into a room of strangers. We search the room for someone who notices us, or somewhere we can safely abide. The new encounter stirs our sensibilities locate our place and people. Until we find them, we feel disoriented and vulnerable. The intensity of those moments reminds us of how much we long for home. A place where we are surely known and included.

When I began as a pastoral counselor, I received a call from a woman nervously asking if she could meet with me. A few days later she came into the office. She was an attractive woman but looked tired and worn. As she sat down it was painfully obvious this was extremely hard for her. Her hands were visibly shaking. So, I asked her, "Where would you like to start?" She searched her mind for what to say. After a long breath she replied, "I don't even know how to broach this topic. Especially with a pastor. So, I'm just gonna say it."

I affirmed her, "Good let's put it on the "workbench," and we'll figure it out together."

She nodded and drew another long breath. Her chin quivered under the strain of the moment. "Well," she said pausing, "I've been married and divorced seven times. Yes, you heard that right-seven times." She hesitated, studying my face to see how I'd handle such news and then continued, "And here's what I want to talk to you about. I want to get married again. Is that a sin?"

Now I paused. Actually, I was praying. I could not help but notice this woman's earnest longing to give and receive love. She embodied that first foundational truth: we all crave love. Although she had not yet experienced the love she yearned for, her heart was still urging her to try again. I answered her, "No, that's no sin." Surprise swept over her face as

I continued, "You are doing what we are designed to do. Find our people and our place. However, you may need some help discovering more helpful ways to find our place and people." Her relief was evident in her posture. She leaned forward with tears in her eyes and said, "So there's something right with me??" "Absolutely!" I assured her. "There's something very right about that desire. Let's talk more about how you can best discover your people and your place."

We spent numerous sessions talking about how we learn to "make love". It became clear she had entered her other marriages ill equipped to love well. But it wasn't too late. She learned. She worked hard, and I'm happy to say she made huge strides in her life and married again.

That kind of transformation is the aim of this book. To help you learn love well. More precisely, to practically equip you to make the love you desire. The reality is that we cannot give what we do not get. We cannot receive what we don't understand. If the families we grew up in were unable to provide that, then we must be intentional about discovering where we can get what we need. It's hard, but good work. In fact, it's the best work we give ourselves to because we are divinely designed to love well. If we weren't it would be a cruel command from our Maker to "love one another."

QUESTIONS:
- Do you have someone who is safe for you to process what you are reading?
- Do you have some people in your life who model for you what good love looks like? What is it they do, or don't do that is inviting to you?

Risking love:

Learning love requires risk and trust. Risk and trust are challenging for us to step into and yet there is no making of love apart from them. They are inseparable in many ways. You won't foster trust if you don't learn to take some risks, and at times the result of your risking is exactly why you pull back on your trust. At first it may sound odd that risk would be so instrumental in love. Especially when we grew up hearing about story book endings where they live happily ever after. But often even those happy story endings were preceded with challenges, changes, struggles and intense learning. Even the fairy tales promote the reality of learning to make love. Oh, how lovely a no-risk venture would be! But love is risky because giving and receiving love is extraordinarily complex. It's been said that "we see the world as we are and not as the whole world is." More simply put, "we like it when the world works like we do." Hence, the way we want to experience love is tailored to who we are and what we like, not crafted for the people we are attempting to love. Our partners will have a different "style" as well. We are most keenly aware of this when relationships begin or change in some way. A large part of letting someone into our "world" (see Figure 1.1) is founded on risking trust.

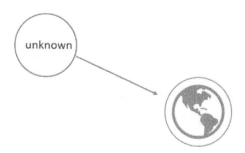

Figure 1.1 (When the unknown moves towards our world)

When we engage a new person (risk) and they reciprocate in a manner that seems good to us, our trust is verified. That boosts our confidence to risk a little more of ourselves in the relationship. This process of risk a little and see what happens is operating continually in our relationships. At some point, the other person is found to be trust-worthy, or not. Risk and trust. They are a package deal.

Brene Brown offers some great help for issuing trust in her book *Dare to Lead*.[1] She uses an acronym BRAVING to communicate trust's critical elements (I have included some comments in italics):

Boundaries: You respect my boundaries, and when you're not clear about what's okay and not okay, you ask. You're willing to say no. *It is essential to respect and honor each spouse's individuality. To push past a person's boundaries screams "this relationship is about ME!"*

Reliability: You do what you say you'll do. Reliability is a critical feature for trust's development. Experts talk about how we crave a sense of predictability from the people we seek to trust. Be real and be honest. Relationally that is not boring, that's reliable.

Accountability: You own your mistakes, apologize, and make amends. Accountability is tied to reliability. If I fail to do what I say or to be who I promised, I work to make amends immediately. Spouses can understand mistakes, but they have a hard time trusting secrets.

Vault: You don't share information or experiences that are not yours to share. One of the simplest ways of demonstrating trustworthiness is keeping information confidential. As partners we share a lot, but one must remember that a person's story is their personal property. Handle with care and confidence!

Integrity: You choose courage over comfort. You choose what is right over what is fun, fast, or easy. And you choose to practice your values rather than simply professing them.

Nonjudgment: I can ask for what I need, and you can ask for what you need. We can talk about how we feel without judgment. We can ask each other for help without judgment.

Generosity: You extend the most generous interpretation possible to the intentions, words, and actions of others.

Now imagine all these elements of trust piled up like a rock pile (figure 1.2). If you pull out integrity, your trust wavers. In fact, if you shift any of these pieces trust will be impacted. Anytime you feel these elements move in your relationship the tendency is to turn down the trust. What you thought about the person or their behavior now seems a little unknown. So, you pull back because your heart is struggling to calculate the meaning of the shift. Are they different because they don't care? Has this changed because our love has? This encounter with new and different always tugs on how much risk we feel we can take in the relationship.

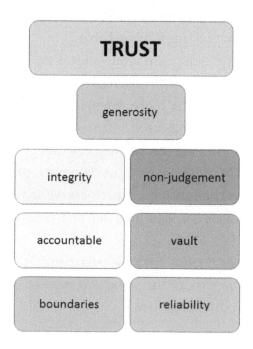

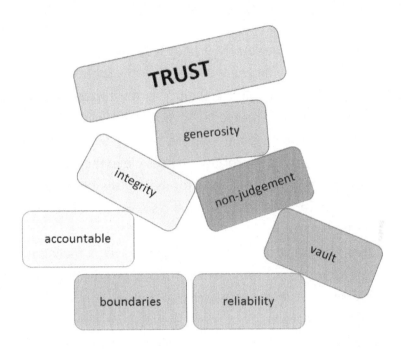

Figure 1.2 (Well-ordered versus disordered trust)

QUESTIONS:

- How do you give trust? Too much too soon or not so fast?
- How do you want to see your capacity to trust grow? Why?
- Do people easily trust you? Why or why not?

The complexity of trust and love becomes evident as we consider how all these elements play into what trust is. No wonder it feels risky. Just one piece shifting creates instability and makes offering love feel extremely risky. Adding to the complexity of this process is the revelation that risk is not just calculated once in a relationship. Life is dynamic. Each day, each of us are learning, growing, and changing. This means both you and your spouse are in for an on-going learning adventure because we are always growing and changing. At times you will encounter new changes and challenges that will surprise you. New knowledge tugs on our trust because we are trying to discern what change means? Is my spouse still reliable and committed to me? Will I still like them? Is my spouse staying up late scheming new ways to drive me crazy? In those kinds of challenges Brown's comments about extending generosity are critical. She encourages us to, "extend the most generous interpretation possible to the intentions, words, and actions of others" which will allow for making the best meaning out of the changes you note.[2] However, in doing so, we can be left wondering, "But will they do that for me?"

All this navigating of trust and risk can leave us feeling frustrated, tired, and confused. It's here where many people will shrink back or give up on the relationship. It feels overwhelming. But we can learn to navigate and learning to navigate helps us make the love we want. However, this also explains why love is hard. The challenge brings us into a critical revelation for our lives. Because, in the midst of this challenging flux our hearts crave someone who is consistent, unchanging and ever reliable. Someone who loves us unconditionally and constantly. Know anyone like that? Enter Jesus. Suddenly amid the chaos of love certain Scriptures appear more relevant. They provide the consistent foundation we crave so we can risk love. Look at Jesus encouraging his friends in Matthew 28:20, "And *surely I am with you always...*" Or James writing in 1:17, "Every good and perfect gift is from above, coming down from the Father of the heavenly lights, *who does not change* like shifting shadows." The writer of Hebrews offers similar encouragements in chapter 13, "God has said, "*Never will I leave you*; never will I forsake you." and "Jesus Christ is the same yesterday and today and forever." These passages encourage us that amid life's turbulent changing there is a Constant One. He will not leave you, fail you or stop loving you. It is the one place where your faith and trust can rest easy. The consistent place we crave is found!

Fostering trust in a Reliable God crafts our "internal safe place." That safe place is a familiar, felt sense that God is entirely reliable and consistently with us while we navigate the ever-changing relational dynamics. Although the world around us is constantly changing there is One within us who is ever the same. When we read the new command of Jesus to "love one another even as I've loved you" (John 13:34) we also need to be assured that "The one who calls you is faithful, and he will do it" (1 Thes. 5:24). Although we hope for our partners to do this for us, the reality is that sometimes it happens and other times it won't. Therefore, the foundation for our practice of love must be grounded on the only One who is perfectly consistent. To place that on anyone else will lead to disappointment, unfulfilled desires, and relational breakdown.

Let's think about this a little more. When there are no current challenges in your relationship it can feel steady like in the diagram below.

Figure 1.3 (No current relational challenges)

But add some of the flux we are talking about and the tension between you rises.

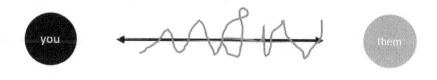

Figure 1.4 (Relational challenges)

In the stress of these seasons you can wonder why your spouse doesn't "get you" or love you like you want. You feel the tug of their demands. The disappointment of their ability to love you unconditionally. You fight with the internal struggle screaming, "why should I try to love and comfort them when they aren't doing the same for me?" The reality is no one can ever love you perfectly except the One who is perfect. Only our relationship with God can supply that (see figure 1.5). We can learn and grow because we are becoming more like Him (see Romans 8:29), yet we will never be as stable or consistent as the One who is Love.

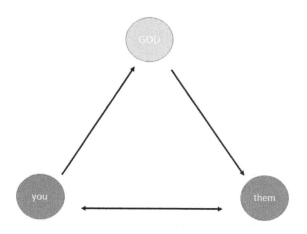

Figure 1.5 (God the source of perfect love)

All this learning and trusting demands we get "comfortable in the uncomfortable". It's how love is made. Your love shouldn't always be uncomfortable, but when challenged you understand everything, we learn is initially uncomfortable. Learning means you are stepping into the unfamiliar. You leave what is familiar, (see Figure 2.1) to venture out into the unknown much like Peter stepping on to the stormy water with Jesus (Mt. 14:22). Fold into this process that you are learning love with another person who is also in varying states of learning, and the anxiety rises. This is why the internal safe place is so critical. Without it one tends to slide back into the known and familiar when they encounter the distress of learning. If you are recognizing these cycles of behavior in your challenges to make love, this is likely why.

It's like when you first learned to ride a bike. Initially it feels incredibly awkward. There can be mishaps and falls. While learning, it's tempting to quit and shout, "I can't do it!" Yet with the encouragement of others and practice most of us learn. Once learned it becomes familiar. We realize we have an inner bike-riding sense. It becomes so well learned we have an adage stating, "it's like riding a bike".

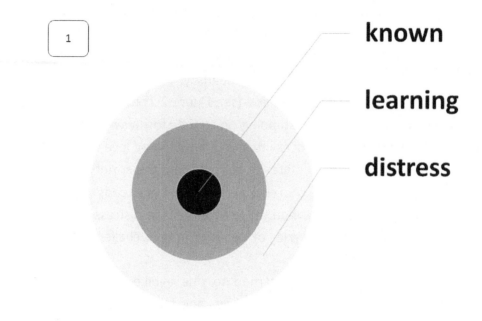

Figure 2.1 (Known, learning and distress zones)

So anytime we have learned something, we have faced uncomfortable challenges and practiced through them to learning. We have left what we know to risk learning what we need. Let's go back to our analogy of learning to ride a bike and consider a few more factors in the learning process.

As you attempt to learn anything you will feel unstable. Instability brings anxiety. When learning to ride it was the balancing and steering of the bike that was tough. You naturally would revert to what you know, i.e. putting your feet down and stopping the bike! But then whoever was teaching you would urge you to peddle a little longer. This felt completely out of control. With a deep breath you would push yourself. Then just when a crash seemed inevitable, they grabbed you and secured the bike. But you pushed yourself a little further. Learning happened. It happened because you risked a little more and trusted your teacher. You stretched yourself in an appropriate way. It wasn't hitting the distress circle, but certainly was outside the known zone. As you practice your learning zone grows. You can picture from the diagrams below: (Figure 2.2-Picture one is your starting point followed by good learning in picture two. Your learning reduces the distress felt while practicing and will eventually become a larger known zone to work from.):

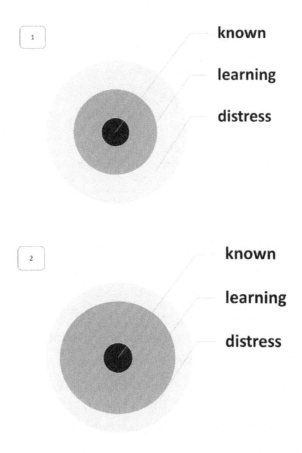

Figure 2.2 (Increasing learning zone)

At this stage, the bike still feels a little wobbly but you're making progress! Your teacher allows you to push yourself a little more. Both of you are noticing that your skills are growing. Soon bike riding begins to feel familiar. You have learned to ride a bike!

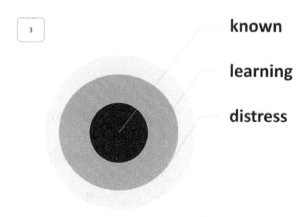

Figure 2.3 (Learning zone enlarges your known zone)

Will there be new challenges as you ride your bike? Yes. Surfaces get slick. Traffic gets busy. New challenges for our learning. Which is why there is always some potential to hit the distress zone.

In like fashion, our capacity to practice good love will face new challenges, which is why we crave something sure and steady: a person who will catch us as we wobble off course. Yet that person cannot do the learning for us. We must risk leaving our known zone. It's our call to get comfortable in the uncomfortable (holding anxiety well). But all the risk is doable because we can trust both Jesus and the people He sends into our lives to catch us when we wobble. This is faith in action!

In Galatians 5:6b Paul declares a whopper of a truth, "...the only thing that counts is faith expressing itself through love." Notice the word faith. Love requires deep functional faith. Faith in the God who says, "I am with you always" and a reasonable level of faith regarding our ability to receive grace and help from Him in our times of need. The surer we become of that, the more confident we will be in extending love towards others. It is as if you have a solid place to put your foot down on as you stretch towards your spouse. The stretching may feel unstable but your foot resting on faith provides enough confidence to risk it. As you practice your capacity to trust your relationship with Christ grows. What you were not able to do on your own becomes possible with His help and the help of others.

QUESTIONS:
- Is learning easy for you? Why or why not?
- How about learning love? Is that easy? Challenging? Confusing?
- What is one thing about love God is teaching you right now?

Approximate learning

While the growth of our faith and learning is primarily our personal responsibility, our mates and family can help the process by practicing "approximate learning". Approximate learning is the phase where we are attempting to learn a new skill but have not grown proficient yet. It's the kid wobbling on the bike. Or your little one who has been steadying themselves on your couch preparing for their first step. This is big news! Imagine with me what the family does as the little one braves their first step. Everyone is on their knees, just far enough away to provoke the step but close enough to catch them when they fall. As the child prepares, they may take their hand off the couch, free-standing for a moment. People cheer! They shout encouragements! Then with all the fanfare surrounding them the babe takes their first attempted step. Even if they fall the crowd cheers and celebrates. Has the baby walked? Not exactly, but everyone is practicing approximate learning. The little one is moving in the right direction and they know it because of all the encouragement and support. Future attempts are right around the corner because of this reassurance. Why do we stop doing this? Such encouragements are needed when we brave "new steps" in life; yet we often find ourselves braving those alone. When traversing the gap of love between two people, wouldn't it be helpful to find your spouse shouting similar encouragements to you as you practiced?

Going back to our bike riding example, we likely received a lot of these approximate encouragements along the way. Things like, "Keep peddling, look straight ahead, you're doing great!" All of these help us to stretch towards better learning. Bike riding is hard, loving is harder.

I encourage couples to note each day the effort made by their partner. It can be a thank you, or "I noticed that...." Or a text, card, or call. Their effort may not be all you hope for but affirm the effort! They are risking. It deserves acknowledgement. These affirmations also help your heart as you highlight their effort to show you love and kindness. These acknowledgments aid each other in the rigorous work of stretching towards each another. What we all hope for is a close connection which looks like this:

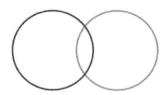

Figure 2.4 (A balanced and shared relationship)

A good shared connection. Each person with equal value and place. No one overworking to maintain the relationship. It's what we hope for in marriage. In practice however, this intimacy is developed in a much more dynamic manner. It happens as we learn to "stretch" towards each other, discovering places of connection and care. Sometimes we find them. Other times our partner must call out hints to help our stretching much like when I played hide and seek with my children. Sometimes they'd feel overwhelmed searching for me and want to give up. But then I'd pretend to sneeze or cough giving them a sound to follow. It helped them find me. When we are missing each other in our efforts to love we need to send a hint or signal to our partners. It helps us 'aim' our love in a more accurate way. At times we need to make clear what we want or need from our partners. It doesn't seem as glamorous as Hollywood portrays it, but you are helping your spouse stretch towards you. As they learn, you may be pleasantly surprised at how talented they become. So realistically this work of connecting looks more like this:

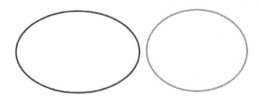

Figure 2.5 (Stretching towards each other relationally)

The art of stretching towards one another is the stuff of love. It is one thing for me to say I love Betsy and quite another to demonstrate my love by how I stretch towards her. Betsy and I are exact opposites on the Meyers/Briggs.[3] She is extroverted and I am quite introverted. She is a high-level thinker and I am a strong feeler. One way we continually practice stretching towards each other is in how we allow for each other's processing. When we both come home from work, we long for two vastly different experiences. I would like quiet and she'd love a conversation! I know as an extrovert Betsy needs to process her day aloud with someone. So here comes the stretch. I've listened all day. My prayer is "Jesus help me be present for Betsy. Give me grace to really listen and enter the conversation." Yet there are other times when I am tired. Perhaps it's been a trying day. Often times I'll seek some quiet in my office. When Betsy comes in, she recognizes the signs. We might talk briefly but she stretches toward me and gives me quiet space. After 37 years we are fairly good at seeing what the other needs. As we stretch towards each other we are offering a tangible, felt "I love you".

So, a significant part of our practice of love is stretching towards our mate in appropriate ways. Appropriate means the stretch is reciprocated or acknowledged by your spouse. Not in a contractual manner that says, I'll give you this if you give me that but rather a mutual commitment to connect. There are times you may need to stretch a little farther. Work a little harder. Just for a season though. Be careful of sliding into a place where your relationship collapses into this:

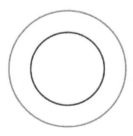

Figure 2.6 (A controlling relationship)

Here the inner person is feeling trapped in this relationship. They are over-working. The relationship has formed around the person's over-accommodation to the other. If not amended, the inner person will "lose themselves" to the relationship. Healthy marriages reciprocate each other's stretch. Typically, we reciprocate one another's stretch more actively when we are courting. Jim was a good friend of mine and a real man's man. One of the things he prided himself on was he never set foot in any shopping malls (not sure why that is manly). Then along came Brenda. Brenda liked to shop. Brenda really liked to shop. Jim really liked Brenda. Guess where stretching took Jim? The mall! Jim still disliked malls, but malls took on a new beauty as long as Brenda was there. Now Brenda enjoyed shopping even more because Jim went with her. But if Brenda begins to insist all they do is shop; the stretch has collapsed. By the way, Brenda had a similar aversion to camping as Jim did to malls. Her aversion was strangely cured during their courtship!

This kind of relational navigation requires us to hold unto ourselves as we reach towards others. Relationships can easily collapse into stretching too much or underworking if we don't have a solid internal safe place. That's the focus of this next chapter.

QUESTIONS:
- How stretched are you feeling right now?
- Who is directing the level of your stretch...you, your spouse or God?
- What would a stretch towards you from your spouse look like right now?

Chapter 2: You Can Only Give What You Got

Hurt people hurt people:

Larry and Sue sat down in my office. You could feel the tension. Trying to be civil, they were obviously frustrated. I started gently: "Where would be a good place to start today?' "Good luck with that" Larry offered, "there is no good place to start with her". "That's so unfair Larry...you act like you are so reasonable. You can't stay in a conversation without screaming and I'm the one who is unreasonable?" Back and forth it went. One hurt person hurting the other who in turn wants to hurt them back. Eye for an eye. The stuff of wars. As a counselor I see it too often.

But how is it two people who met, dated, got to know each other well enough to decide to spend their life together, plan a wedding, do a wedding; end up here? It's a collision of needs, hurts and history. What's being revealed to you is what needs to be learned and healed. The struggle in this relationship started many relationships back in their history. Places where someone didn't care for them. Someone didn't help them. It leaves scars. It also leaves big gaps when trying to navigate all the nuances of a close relationship.

Understanding attachments:

John Bowlby is the father of Attachment Theory. He worked to explain how we develop an inner working model of relating (this basic concept is part of what I talk about when describing an inner safe place).[1]

Adult attachment designates three main "attachment styles," or manners in which people perceive and respond to intimacy in romantic relationships, which parallel those found in children: Secure, Anxious, and Avoidant. Basically, secure people feel comfortable with intimacy and are usually warm and loving; anxious people crave intimacy, are often preoccupied with their relationships, and tend to worry about their partner's ability to love them back; avoidant people equate intimacy with a loss of independence and constantly try to minimize closeness. In addition, people with each of these attachment styles differ in: their view of intimacy and togetherness the way they deal with conflict their attitude toward sex their ability to communicate their wishes and needs their expectations from their partner and the relationship. [2]

Bowlby's theory of attachment can be pictured like this (Figure 3.1):

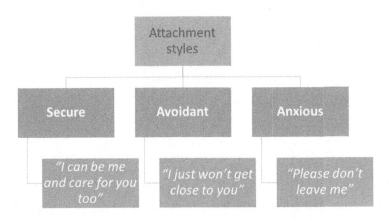

Figure 3.1 (Attachment styles at a glance)

Basically, Bowlby's theory says if as a child you experienced a positive and loving caregiver, you would in turn learn how to relate to others in a similar fashion. The secure and nurturing relationship would foster what Bowlby called a "secure attachment" (see Figure 3.2). These folks have a settled and learned sense of self in relationships which allows them to be emotionally vulnerable and available to others. Basically, they are comfortable depending on others and having others depend on them. They have a healthy balance between intimacy and independence. You'll note in following the diagram there emerges a little space between the couple during the response phase. It's indicating a space that acknowledges difference and uniqueness. We never stop being an individual. When working securely we find a place where we are willing to share "me" to make the "we". Love is a deliberate gift. I choose to give me. Their relational inheritance has nurtured an inner person who has learned foundational interpersonal skills.

SECURE

Figure 3.2 (A Secure attachment)

Avoidant

A person who has learned an Avoidant style of connection feels threatened by the vulnerability required in intimate relationships. So, they disengage saying something like, "meh, I don't care." But they do, we all do. They may explain their distance saying, "I need my independence" or "I really don't want people depending on me". When relational challenges come, they go quiet and withdraw. The more intense the difficulty the more likely they will conceal their feelings. The deeper the hurt the wider the distance. Calm only comes when they are away from the relationship. Distance is their partner. While the securely attached person had people help them navigate challenges, a dismissively attached person likely was left alone or unattended to. If you rarely experienced someone coming to care for you in the testy moments of life, you have no sense of expecting it now.

AVOIDANT

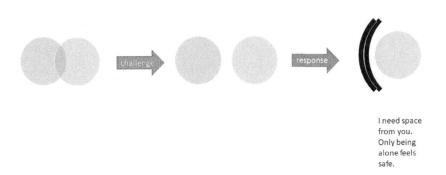

I need space
from you.
Only being
alone feels
safe.

Figure 3.3 (An Avoidant attachment)

Anxious

The Anxiously attached person feels the need for close relationships, but when working for "we" they grow anxious and unsure. Their response is "come here, no, go away". They say things like, "I want to be close, but I don't know if they could love someone like me." Often Anxiously attached people have deep pain or trauma in their history. Past caregivers may have helped them but then confusingly hurt them at other junctures. This creates a lot of anxiety relationally. They don't know whether they will get good or bad help. Therefore, any current relational tests can trigger past pain. As it does, they feel smaller and less able than their partner. Impaired by their uncertainty, their responses turn erratic and inconsistent. One person mentioned to me, "I feel like the squirrel in the middle of the road. I don't know what to do...move towards them or run away."

ANXIOUS

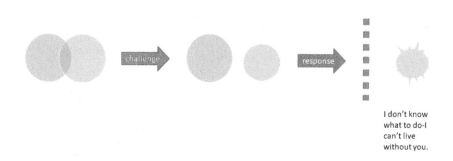

I don't know
what to do-I
can't live
without you.

Figure 3.4 (An Anxious attachment)

This can all sound so "clinical". Anxious, avoidant, and secure. Do not lose heart here. This is not a Psychology 101 final exam. What has been most helpful to me and the people I've worked with is to note our reactions to relational challenges. I use the word "reaction" intentionally. Our learned love style will react to our spouses when tried. There will be an inner reaction- how it feels to us and an outer response- what we do because of that feeling.

When I've shared my story with others, I describe my inner reaction as a "puffer fish". You know those goofy looking fish that blow up like a car's activated air bag when challenged. So, if Betsy and I would bump into a perceived conflict it felt (my inner reaction) too close; I'd react like a puffer fish. Bam. My emotions would just blow up. I couldn't think clearly. I felt threatened. All I wanted to do was run. Running was my outer response to an inner fear. In all my previous close relationships, I ran. In learning love, I never in those moments analyzed what attachment style I was. Nope, I'd focus on the basic skills helping me to stay in the moment. Breath. Practice calm. Look to Jesus to settle me. I'd deactivate my inner puffer fish! It's those basic but powerful practices that will help us stay calm and present during the learning of love.

Here's a glance at those three attachment styles and how they may respond relationally (Figure 3.6):

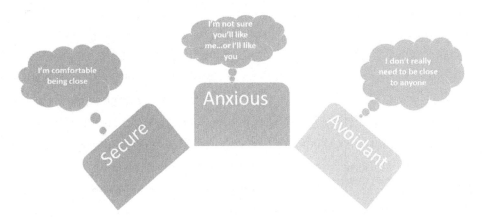

Figure 3.6 (Typical attachment responses)

QUESTIONS:
- As you read about the different attachment styles is there one that sounds more like you?
- If you landed some place other than "secure", take heart. If you'd known me at the start of my story, you'd have never guessed I'd become a pastor and marriage counselor. You learned a style in the past so you can surely learn a different one now. Trust me.

- If you haven't been able to identify your love style think in terms of just your marriage. Marriage is the most intense "learning lab" of all relationships. How do you respond when your spouse questions you? Challenges you? Disagrees with you?

Learning a new way of love

These styles of attachments are not hard fast categories you are imprisoned by. Rather they are human reactions to the type of care we did or didn't receive. We have just one "me" and when our "me" is neglected we must have some way of responding. Uncoached and unnurtured we will likely wind up becoming aloof, anxious, or too compromising. One of the simplest ways to discern that you are sliding out of a secure attachment is when you're overworking to save your "me". You become defensive or counterattack. Now you are not fighting for the "we" but struggling to save the "me". Overworking shows up in our withdrawing, counterattacking, sarcasm, and stonewalling. All these, and others, are signs we are threatened. Working from fear will not be helpful. On the other hand, this doesn't mean you shouldn't ever express your wants or needs. A securely attached person can be very clear about what they need but they will not let the unsettled, insecure "me" drive their responses. You have needs and wants. Many of those are valid. They need to be shared. But "sharing" meets working together in the relationship to create a mutually satisfying place for both of you.

Also please keep in mind that your attachment style is not an indictment on your parents. They gave you what they got. It is likely their history and story had gaps of care. They too were left to care for their "me" in less than helpful ways. Holding a grudge will do little to help you in your quest to love. In fact, it will tether you to them in an unhelpful way. Instead of being free to learn love, you are bound to your reactions to what hurt you. So, in the wake of this human struggle what hope is there?

Enter Jesus with His great promise, "I have come that they may have life, and have it to the full." (John 10:10) As a former Anxiously attached person, I want to encourage you that change, and growth is possible! Jesus' promise brought hope and love to me. One of the great blessings of our design is; although we may not have gotten what we needed to learn love as children, we have the present capacity to heal and learn now. I've watched hundreds of people recraft their relational style and enjoy a "full life". When you watch someone change a habit, begin to exercise, or learn an instrument; it is a testament of this potential.

One further thought regarding attachment. You may be the individual who has learned a secure style and are married or relating to someone who is yet learning. Take heart! I suspect God often calls us to be "missionaries of love". My wife Betsy was one of these people for me when we first married. There were some essential gifts she offered me helping me grow in my capacity to love. Here is a short list:

- She did not "over-love" but was consistent in her care for me. Over loving involves rescuing a person or dismissing a person from their share of the work. This can be crippling to them and to your relationship.

- She was not demanding of more than I could offer. To me, this was miraculous. I never felt Betsy judge me or sigh over my inabilities. She recognized my efforts and the places I was learning. She also discovered how to partner with Jesus in a grace-filled manner as she walked with me. All of this created a safe and big space for me to learn. There was no pressure from her to hurry up. This was our journey together in making love.

- Betsy has told me how grateful she was to know I was meeting with our pastor and another mentor to continue to learn and grow. Instead of bearing the weight of my learning on her solitary shoulders, it was shared with a group of people. Learning love is best done with a handful of people. We are meant to discover our people and our place.

QUESTIONS:
- As you finish reading this section pause for moment. Think with me.
    - What stands out to you?
    - What's clearest in your mind?
    - How are you feeling right now? (not thinking but feeling.)
    - What do you need?
- Does Jesus' promise to give life to the full seem real to you?
- Is there anything you want to talk through with someone right now?

How we form

John Bowlby discerned our relational capacity/style is greatly impacted by our family of origin, but it's not a dead-end for our development. Once you understand what you received or didn't get, we can target learning the skills you need to have healthier relationships. One way to discover this is by drawing a family map or genogram.

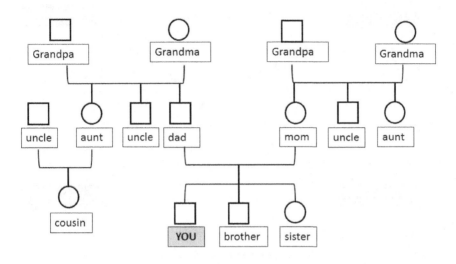

Figure 3.7 (An example genogram)

This family tree helps you understand how love was defined and practiced in your family. This can be difficult to revisit so consider processing this with someone safe to you. It may be your spouse, friend, pastor, or counselor but there is something vital to the process in having people with you. Once your family is mapped out, answer the questions provided at the end of this chapter. Keep in mind we are sifting through our family story to discover what we need to learn. Dr. Dan Siegel says plainly, "If you can make sense of your story, you can change it."[3]

Our stories and lives are largely a product of two elements:

1. The people in our lives.
2. The experiences in our lives.

Therefore, you can experience significant help by intentionally importing new relationships and experiences. These are the stuff of life. The diagram below depicts this formation matrix:

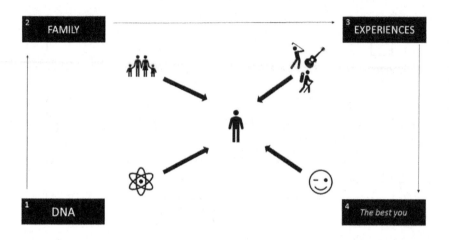

Figure 3.8 (Personal formation matrix)

Every person begins life inheriting this "seed" of a person called DNA. But DNA isn't the only factor in our development. You are "planted" in a family of origin which has a forming impact on you. We've discussed how those relationships impact your person and relational style. Those relationships also propel you into certain experiences. If your mom or dad noticed you were talented in music, they may have encouraged you to keep plunking on the family piano. Such encouragement might nudge you towards more musical experiences and training. Eventually you could be performing at Carnegie Hall. It would be the culmination of how these factors shaped and formed you. This is incredibly hopeful because we are not human "dones", but rather "human becomings"!

You can see the genius of God at work when you consider the potential help of Christian fellowship and church. Mentors and models can have a life-giving impact on your relational capacity. As a young dad I realized this. Feeling insecure about my abilities as a dad I knew I needed encouragement. So, every Sunday after service I would walk down to where the Sunday school kids were. I'd search the hall for dads and wait to see which kids would sprint to their fathers with joy and a shout, "Dad!". Those were the dads I knew I needed to talk to. So, I'd ask them to spend some time with me talking about parenting. Many of them had lasting impacts on my ability to father and I'm extremely grateful for their help. In so many ways we are a product of the people we are around. Being intentional and prayerful about surrounding yourself with people who can help you learn love is paramount.

Furthermore, you see the Lord promising to surround you with new family in passages like Psalm 68:6, "God sets the lonely in families." So be watchful and prayerful for who He might send your way. He is working on your behalf!

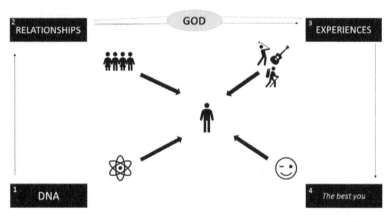

Figure 3.9 (Spiritually directed formation)

Bob slid down in his chair with a long sigh. "I still hear his voice right here" he said pointing at the side of his head. "Screaming you're a loser! A big loser! You'll always be a loser!" Bob was stuck in time. Despite being a successful businessman Bob, who was now in his 60's, was still hoping to hear different things from a dad who had been dead over 15 years.

Scripture says, "reckless words pierce like a sword" (Proverbs 12:18). Bob's dad had cut deep. Bob confided later in the conversation, "I've been the same way to my kids. I have a lot of regret for the terrible things I've shouted at them. Why do I do that?" "Unfortunately, we give what we got. Sometimes that perpetuates the pain. It's why we say, 'hurt people hurt people'" I offered.

We began the process of sorting through his family history (see the genogram questions in the appendix), exercising forgiveness and intentionally focusing on new relationships and experiences. Part of what we did was to think carefully about the people closest to Bob and determine if there were other models and mentors he needed. Using this grid (Figure 4.0) helped him think through who he needed:

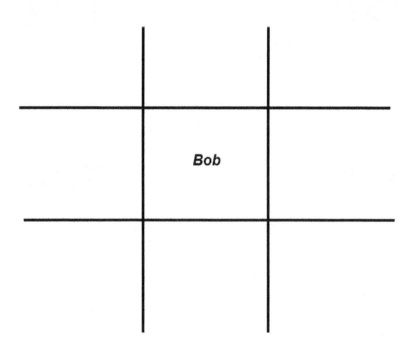

Figure 4.0 (A relationship grid)

We put Bob in the middle of the grid and began to think of the people he needed to have help him learn love. Now, put yourself in the middle of the grid. First include the people who are around you now. How are they helping or hampering your learning love? Then consider what skills or qualities you need to learn most right now. Things like patience, joy, compassion, and understanding. Who do you know that embodies one or more of these qualities? Invite them into your grid. Each box represents a window into your life. No one sees all of you. You don't even see all of you.

Now if we are inviting people into places where we want them to see us (like me wanting help with fathering) they can be a source of helpful growth or at times, pain. Being intentional about these relationships is essential and part of this intentionality involves drawing healthy boundaries.

Boundaries

Boundaries make clear to yourself and others what is okay and what is not okay. It's the line defining ownership. That is mine, this is yours. When you look at the grid in the above illustration, boundaries naturally form around the frames of the grid. When you invite people into your life, you can be clear about what's okay and what's not okay. For example, when you risk confiding in a person, you are trusting them to hold your story. If they break confidence that is a boundary issue. You trusted them with a piece of you and they misused it. They crossed a boundary. It doesn't mean you must completely cut them out of your life. You can have a hard and honest conversation expressing your disappointment. Forgiveness can be exercised, and trust restored. However, that can only happen if the boundary is acknowledged and restoration is made.

God sends people to us:

Beyond our initiation, we should be watching for who God is sending into our life. People who model, encourage, and support our growth. (Figure 4.1)

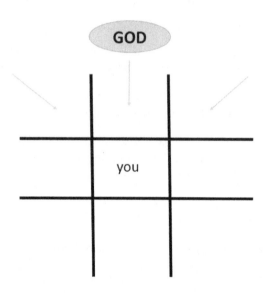

Figure 4.1 (Watching for who God is sending into your life)

QUESTIONS:

- Thinking through our family and relationships can try our hearts. There is such great potential for people to do good in our lives, but when things work out otherwise, it can be excruciating. How is your heart doing?
- What emotions arise when you think about inviting others into your life?
- Each square on the grid represents a window into your life. These windows can be defined by boundaries we set. What are yours? Think about what is ok and not ok for you.

Each of us has a "relational inheritance". These people had a forming influence on who you became and how you related to others. Going back to Bob, he was reckoning with his relational inheritance. Not to place blame, but to discern what he needed to learn. Understanding that inheritance helped him intentionally build a "new family" around him. It is important for you as well. Yet as helpful as this "new family" can be, there is a place where faith and grace have to help us do what we cannot do for ourselves.

God uses people!

It is critical to understand the importance of allowing God to use safe people in our lives. Discipleship is not just a "neat God idea." We learn relating from relationships. Whether you are secure or otherwise in your current relational capacity, you are living proof of this. I've watched many people struggling with attachment attempt to develop healthier patterns on their own. This is not possible! If you are going to learn healthier relating, you will need to do so by risking new relationships.

One time, Betsy and I were having our communication time. We were winding things up when I took a deep breath and risked asking, "is there anything you've been waiting to talk to me about?" I personally structured our time this way because of my "puffer fish" tendencies. If we hit anything too emotionally charged for me at the onset, I'd be emotionally done for the evening. Betsy shifted in her chair and very gently answered, "Yes I've been thinking about something." My inner puffer fish was quivering with anticipation! I took another breath and settled myself. Betsy continued surprising me with a generous list of how I was such a good husband. Then she said, "James Dobson of Focus on the Family would give you an A. You do so many things right. But it feels like we're missing romance." I remember thinking to myself, "Dobson would give me an "A" and you want romance?!" The reality was that romance really meant vulnerability. Betsy clarified, "What I want is you. You. I feel like what I get is what you do, but not you." It took a while but eventually I caught on. In practice what I had done was created my "safe distance" by doing what was obviously right as a husband. You can do the right things and still not be in it. I did that. I see others attempt that as well.

Now I was in a dilemma. I could read a book instructing me to pray for my wife. Check. Did that. I could listen to sermons urging me to listen to my wife. Check. Did that. But how in the world does a guy risk giving himself away? I didn't need a book; I needed an example. So, I prayed, "God, send some people to help me." He did. Living examples of what I needed to learn. They modeled it for me and engaged me in long conversations which were immensely helpful. Until then, my inner sense was "Don't give too much of yourself away, you'll get burned. Give just enough to get by." But these guys modeled a new possibility for me. They risked! Seeing them practice transformed my older beliefs into a new way of relating. Having good information (Figure 4.2) wasn't enough. I needed models and interaction. You do too. We all do. It's incredibly important for you to realize in this journey of making love. I can't think of any other area more intricate than marriage and yet we get very little coaching in how to do it. We don't want to parrot what others do, but please understand we learn relating by relating.

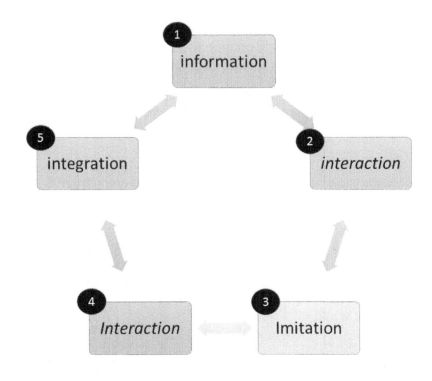

Figure 4.2 (Dynamics of learning new behaviors)

Thinking about learning:

Think with me as you view the diagram above. Much of our learning as youths came from imitation. We'd read books, take notes and listen to lectures. But much of the information lacks a fuller picture of what it really looks like to live out the information out. Earlier in the book, we talked about learning to ride a bike. How would it work for you if I gave you a book full of information about bike riding but never showed you a picture of a bike or someone riding one? The information would be incomplete. You need to see something more to complete the picture your mind is forming around the text you're reading. It's no different with learning love. You need to see a picture, a person modeling love; to help your learning be complete. Furthermore, having opportunities to interact with this living model helps us incorporate information much more readily. As in learning to ride the bike, they can give helpful feedback to our process by shouting, "Pedal faster! Don't lean to the right!" Those interactions help us fill out our learning and move towards real life integration.

QUESTIONS:
- Do you know some couples who appear happy together?
    - If so, how do you know they are happy?
        - What do you observe?
        - Are there things they do/say you wish were in your marriage?

Chapter 3: Jesus The Safe Place

If I love him like that, who will love me?

I had just posed several questions to Sheila which led her to an epiphany. She saw clearly when Mark did what she liked, she loved him freely. Conversely, when he failed her-she withheld love. Sheila then asked me, "What can I do differently?" I paused to think. Answering, I suggested, "What do you think would happen if you loved him no matter what?" She froze. It was a deeply theological moment. Her response came with a wave of apparent anxiety, "If I love him like that, who will love me?"

It's the million-dollar question, isn't it? If I love them like that, with no reservation or strings attached; who will love me? We are finite, and we know it. Our patience, kindness, and love all have limits. They run out. Usually when they do, we are exasperated and exhausted. We've given all we can. We feel like we are losing "me". It begins like this (Figure 4.3):

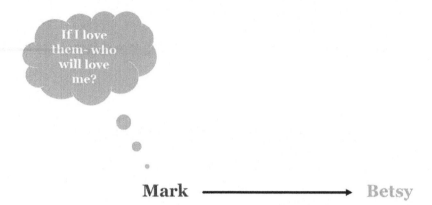

Figure 4.3 (Running out relationally)

When Betsy begins to ask for my help or needs me to listen, I must give a part of myself. At first the demand isn't felt so strongly (see Figure 4.4).

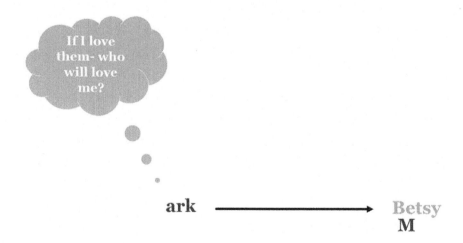

Figure 4.4 (Running low relationally)

But now let's say Betsy needs something more of me.

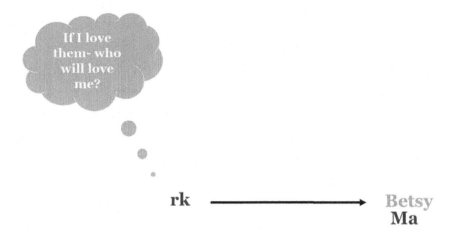

Figure 4.5 (Increasing lack of capacity)

At this point (Figure 4.5) I am feeling the strain. I'm giving a lot of me to her and beginning to feel the drain. It continues...

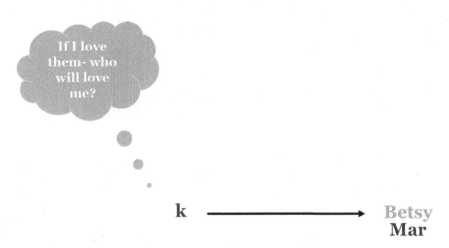

Figure 4.6 (Full on panic! I can't give anymore!)

Now, I panic (Figure 4.6). I've given all I can. My limit has been reached. The cry from the deepest parts of me is "if I love Betsy like this, who will love me?!" Stop and think about this. Every person in every relationship is finite. Everyone has limits. What we crave is someone who never runs out, is always available and is always loving. Know anyone like that? Obviously, it is this God who says, "I will never leave you or forsake you." Furthermore, the words of Jesus in John 15:9 make great sense here, "As the Father has loved me, so have I loved you. Now remain in my love." This is prefaced by his new command, "My command is this: Love each other *as I have loved you*." (John 15:9-italics mine). This is not religious jargon; this is practical wisdom to help us love. You see as I give myself to Betsy, I can do it in concert with God's guidance and grace. I can trust Him to give me the ability and the power. His infinite grace fills the gap of my finite capacity to give. It looks like this (Figure 4.7):

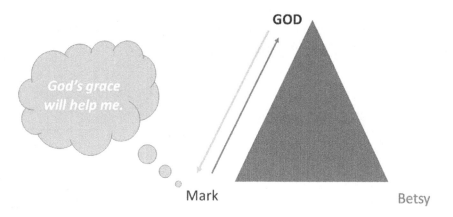

"...casting all your anxieties on him, because he cares for you."

1 peter 5.7

Figure 4.7 (My limitations meet God's infinite grace)

QUESTIONS:

- This is an essential part of learning love. Think with me. Have you experienced places in your life where you encountered God's grace helping you do what you should do but couldn't do on your own?
- In your prayer life do you practice both elements of 1 Peter 5:7? First, casting your cares upon Him and secondly, receiving His care about those concerns? What does your own practice of faith look like presently?
- Do you have a growing sense and connection to God's love for you?

Answering love's biggest question:

The answer to my need, your need and Sheila's question, "who will love me?" is found in the promise of the One who is faithful. His grace is sufficient. However, His grace isn't instant. Oh, that we could receive grace like a quick trip through the drive thru. But love is patient (I Cor. 13.4) which translates to, sometimes I must wait. Therefore, one of the most critical skills in loving well is learning to "put ourselves on hold". This takes practice. This calls for prayer. This is beyond us. We need grace! Yet when I encounter God's grace to wait and give myself freely to Betsy, I discover in a very real way the One who will love me if I love others like that. This is part of crafting an inner safe self. It is not a solitary exercise, but rather a teaming with the Unlimited God who promises to be "with us always".

QUESTIONS:

- Why do you suppose patience is the first item Paul lists in his definition of love?
- How do you do with "putting yourself on hold"?

- When do you know it's time to put yourself on hold? How do you know it's not time for patience?
- Why do you think God has us wait?

The Inner Safe Self

In the beginning it was not like it is now. There in the garden the first couple experienced the beauty of an unforced, easy vulnerability and trust towards one another. "Adam and his wife were both naked, and they felt no shame" (Genesis 2:25). It's hard to comprehend in today's world. Today, there are the whispers in the workplace. Murmurs in the hallways of schools. Times when a good friend betrays you on the one thing you asked them to keep quiet. "Never again" you tell yourself. It all advises us to keep safe and go it alone. Can we ever recover a sliver of what Genesis reports Adam and Eve experiencing? The incredible freedom of being vulnerable but not ashamed, mocked, or ridiculed. Yes, we can. It was why dying was a joy set before Jesus. He's made a way and He's going to make a way for us now. It will require our utmost trust in Him who is Faithful. It will demand our surrender of a well-practiced lifestyle of going solo and hiding in the shadows. But it is possible. I'm one who has been drawn out of hiding.

It's not just you anymore

All relationships involve places where we bump into different. Different is unsettling to us. We like known. Known and familiar are similar in how they impact us relationally. When I meet someone for the first time and move past the initial hesitancy to engage in a conversation; that conversation can land in an uncomfortable/different place. I could discover the person is severely prejudiced and quite self-righteous about it. That is a significant difference to me (see Figure 4.8). It is not part of my known zone. Most of my sensibilities will be sounding an alarm that screams inside me, "Run away this person is strange!".

The only way most of us will feel safe again is to create distance from that uncomfortable individual. It looks like this (Figure 4.8):

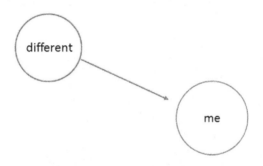

Figure 4.8 (When different invades my world)

When anyone or anything different approaches my world, I feel uncomfortable. Uncomfortable often equals threatened. So, I retreat and wall off (see Figure 4.9). The weirder the encounter, the more distance I desire and the bigger wall I create:

Figure 4.9 (Our response to different: distance and a wall)

It's not just me practicing this when I encounter different or strange. It's largely a normal human experience. This is our well-practiced reaction to awkward encounters on this planet. Instead of 'naked and unashamed and together' we do, 'exposed, shame on you and I'm outta here." When our spouse does something to us that feels different or strange, our natural reaction is "expose, shame, and reject". That builds walls and isolation in our marriages.

QUESTIONS:

- What do you do when you encounter different?
- How about when your spouse does/says something different to you?
- What would it look like for you to move towards "different" with Jesus leading the way?

Giving and receiving grace:

Now when Jesus steps into your life He brings with Him a savvy about reaching different and difficult people. You and I were once on the other side of that wall. He reached past our awkwardness and loved us. He traversed the gap of difference. He then urges us to, "love our enemies" or "If you love those who love you, what credit is that to you? Even sinners love those who love them" (Luke 6:32). This is absolutely terrifying if we think we must do that apart from Him. Therefore, Jesus says plainly, 'apart from me you can do nothing...' (John 15:5). He, of course, is referring directly to being able to love like He does. It's impossible without Him. So, when I am talking about an "inner safe place" I am referring not to a singular just me thing, but rather a ***practiced*** trust in Jesus and me.

This is what all the strange verbiage is about in the New Testament. This idea of "abiding" in Christ. How does one do that? Paul later reduces it to a simple but challenging command to be "in" Him. Either these notions are religious jargon, or they have direct relevance to our practice of life and love. It's probably obvious to you where I stand. Here is why.

I became a believer at the age of 23. I was unchurched and troubled. No one knew the depth of my internal struggles. After all, I managed to graduate from college. That amazed my family! I worked on the residential life staff of a successful private college. That meant that I had to navigate a huge number of relationships. On the outside, things looked pretty good. Fairly normal. Yet internally I was unable to get close to anyone. I had lots of "friends", but I kept them at a safe and manageable distance. I could be the 'life of the party' if I needed to, but that was just me pretending to be someone I thought they may like. The real Mark was painfully insecure. In relationships that required I show the real me, I fled like a bandit.

Then I met Christ. In that first encounter, I collided with the incredible love of God. I had never experienced anything like that. I stayed up all night talking to this new Father of mine confessing my sins, struggles and fears. Believe me, it took all night. Friends and family were struck by the dramatic change in my life. Indeed, some things changed miraculously; but my internal struggles with relationships remained. Two years later I met and married my wife Betsy. I admired her demeanor with others. She was calm and relaxed in relationships. Wow! I needed that, so why not get married, right?

That first year was a particularly challenging one for me. Every other adult relationship had an escape route. I could distance myself. I could hide things. Cover up was easy. Marriage had me trapped. Intensifying all of this was the church we were in. There were many young married couples wanting to spend time with us. It was exhausting. One evening Betsy answered the phone and it was a couple inviting us out to dinner. In my panic I responded grumpily, "Well, if you really want to go." I was stuck. I didn't want to disappoint Betsy but that meant facing the terror of being around others who may detect the real me. Betsy wisely asked the people if she could call them in a bit and hung up. She sat down next to me and asked, "Mark what's wrong?" Here's where God inside of me helped incredibly. Mark on his own would have answered the usual, "Nothing I'm fine." But God nudged me to be honest. More honest than I've ever been. "Well, I don't know Bets. I just freeze up. I want to be a nice person like you, but if I'm honest- it terrifies me. I don't know what to do, what to say and I'm afraid they won't like me if they really get to know me." I couldn't believe I was saying this. In fact, I was never able to wrap words around it before. Betsy nodded and asked, "Is there anything I can do?" The old Mark Spencer would have declared, "No, I'll just have to figure it out" (hear that? It's alone and away again). But once again God was stirring me to be open, honest, and vulnerable. "Well, I'd like you to be sure that I don't want to be this way. I'm meeting with our pastor and working on what I can. It just doesn't come easy for me." Betsy assured me that she saw my hard work. "And you can pray for me." I added. She smiled and said, "I am". Then I offered something that I am sure was divinely inspired, "You know it would help me if you could find it in your heart to just let me say yes or no without you showing disappointment. When I sense you're let down I just want to suck it up and do it. I really feel trapped when that happens." Even as I write this, I can't believe I said it. Betsy has heard me tell this story dozens of times and dozens of times she has said, "Mark, that was easy for me. God's grace was in that."

Over the next two years Betsy graciously gave me a grace space. She said she could see how hard I was working. I was. But not just me, Christ in me. Jesus had been helping me grow and learn in very practical ways. His presence and grace were obvious to me, so I risked more conversations and dropped my guard. It was slow but good work. The shaky, fearful insides of Mark Spencer were being transformed. That transformation was possible because I learned to trust Christ in me and the good people he had put around me. I needed both. You do too. Without that kind of support, you can't risk love.

QUESTIONS:

- Are there any parts of my story that resonate with you? If so, how is God inviting you to trust Him with that?
- God may be calling you to be a "Betsy" to your spouse who is a bit like "Mark". How does that land with you?
- In your relationship with God, is it relatively easy for you to recognize when He is "nudging" you to risk?

You and I work from a composite of life experience. All our relational history forges an inner model of how we will presently relate to others. For those of us who did not receive good coaching, that model probably will look a little like mine. Looking good on the outside but struggling internally. Perhaps working hard to please, deceive, or manipulate people. Not trying to be mean, but simply trying to survive. Doing whatever we think we need to do to protect ourselves. But that's Christ's job, not ours. If we settle that, we can settle a lot. With all the ambivalence of relationships you simply cannot rely on them to provide the stability you crave. It must come from Jesus within you because what is around you is uncertain and at times unsafe.

In Jesus' most desperate moments we learn how His inner safe place sustained Him. "To this you were called, because Christ suffered for you, leaving you an example, that you should follow in his steps. He committed no sin, and no deceit was found in his mouth. When they hurled their insults at him, he did not retaliate; when he suffered, he made no threats. Instead, he entrusted himself to him who judges justly." (1 Pe. 2:21-23).

This is one of the most incredible passages about Jesus' practice of love. He is enduring incredible and unjust suffering by the people He came to save. They offer no help, only insults and ridicule. How does Jesus respond? No reaction. No retaliation. No fighting fire with fire. How does He do that? Peter writes, "Instead, He entrusted Himself to Him who judges justly" (1 Peter 2:23).

Now keep in mind that Jesus has done this to provide us with a clear example (1 Peter 2:21). Thankfully, we don't face the horror of crucifixion, but we sure encounter insults and misunderstandings, don't we? When that happens, how do you respond? I know what I do too often. I resort to another outdated passage: "an eye for an eye". Then I remember, "Christ suffered for you, leaving you an example, that you should follow in his steps." Follow in his steps. Hmmm.

Peter goes on in verse 7 to call us married couples, "joint heirs of grace". Why does he say that? It's because only through grace can you live like that. Grace is that gift that helps us "do what we know we should do and can't do on our own." That grace is discovered when we live out of our relationship with Christ as depicted in the diagram (Figure 5.0) below:

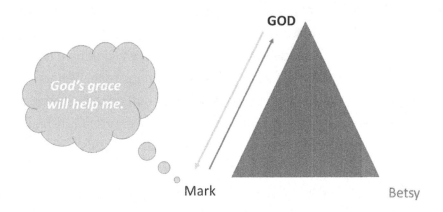

Figure 5.0 (Casting your cares and receiving God's care for you)

Peter is coaching us to cast our anxiety on Him who cares for us. When we are struggling relationally, we are wrestling with that core question of "who is going to love me?" When we've been insulted or mistreated, it produces deep levels of anxiety within us. Now, what will we do with that anxiety? Will we lash out and retaliate? Or will we follow the Lamb and entrust our cares to Him? But it's not just casting cares that Peter is concerned with. He wants us to experience God's care for whatever is troubling us. That is what frees us. The awareness that not only has God shouldered our cares, but he is extending real care to us. Peace in a tumultuous time. Grace to bear with the unbearable. Joy in a season of hardship. Now our cares don't drive our response, but rather the care of our Father.

This is foundational. When John writes, 'we love because He first loved us' (1 Jn. 4:19) he is clueing us into a reality. We must learn to carry an on-going sense of God's presence into the midst of our relational challenges. This means learning how to quiet oneself, waiting patiently for your spouse, and listening for what is wisdom in your situation. These are things we likely hope our spouse would do for us, so why don't we do them for ourselves? The answer likely lies in our attachment style. When one is reared in a secure environment, they are afforded sufficient nurturing that helps them discern a healthy balance of give and take in relationships. In sum, we learn how to care for self as well as others. If this hasn't been learned it needs to be, otherwise there is an imbalanced hope that your partner will care for you like you wish you would care for you.

Sue's head looked down as she announced, "Mike just doesn't get me." "What doesn't he get?" I asked. "Me" she stated flatly. "I have to tell him everything." "Everything?" I queried. "Yes. He doesn't know what I need." I asked, "Do you tell him what you need?" "Usually not. I mean, isn't that what a good partner does; know what you need?"

It is fair to hope that your partner will grow in the knowledge of who you are and what you would like. However, that knowledge often comes by way of you asking for what you want. Asking for what you want requires a willingness to be vulnerable. Vulnerability demands a secure sense of self, saying that your request matters and is appropriate. Sue's hopes were understandable but off that mark. She needed to risk honesty by telling Mike what she was looking for in the relationship. However, given Sue's history she never learned that, especially in the intensity of a close relationship. I asked Sue, "Do you ask for what you want in other relationships?" She thought for a moment. "With some friends I do. Like I'll say I don't want to eat there. That kind of thing." So, I continued, "What is different between those moments and asking Mike?" Her face froze for a moment. "I expect Mike to know me, to know all about me." "Uh huh. And how will Mike know you if you don't help him by letting him know you don't want to eat at that restaurant?" She blurted out, "But I feel so picky, like a diva when I say those things." This is the kind of big gap we feel when we've not had enough practice learning how to ask for what's appropriate in a relationship. You can see her dilemma. Either I ask for what I want, which makes me a diva, or I swallow my wishes in the outside hope that Mike will take care of them. When we are learning these relational skills, they can feel like Grand Canyon sized gaps. It is exceedingly difficult to navigate a good space when you haven't had the equipping in your youth. There are four sources that can help us negotiate the ambivalence of these spaces:

1. God's Spirit helping guide us.
2. Good instruction from books and other sources.
3. Mentors and models who show us what navigating these spaces looks like in real life and relationships.
4. Well-paced conversations with your spouse.

QUESTIONS:

- Who do you feel like in your marriage: Mike or Sue?
- Both Mike and Sue have legitimate desires. You do too. What are yours? What is the Lord saying to you about them?
- As you think about addressing your desires, does it feel like that giant space that's hard to navigate? As you read the next section be watching for what you might need (God's guidance, helpful instruction, a mentor, or process time with your spouse.)

God's guidance

You've probably heard someone ask a friend, "What's that little voice inside you saying?" Sue wished she could put a little voice inside of Mike that would tell him all her wishes. That sounds outrageous, but when you consider God's plan, maybe not. He has placed His Spirit inside of us. Jesus tells us "the Advocate, the Holy Spirit, whom the Father will send in my name, will teach you all things and will remind you of everything I have said to you" (John 14:26). Later Jesus expounds on this by saying, "But when he, the Spirit of truth, comes, he will guide you into all the truth" (John 16:13). Most of the Spirit's efforts are to guide us in a way so that God's fruit is born in our lives. If the chief command of Jesus is to "love one another. As I have loved you, so you must love one another" (John 13:34), then we can be sure that Jesus wants us to be successful at that love. This is why Paul writes in Galatians 5:22-23, "But the fruit of the Spirit is love, joy, peace, patience, kindness, goodness, faithfulness, gentleness and self-control." Aren't these the stuff of good relationships? All of God's resources and the Spirit within you are laboring towards this end. The most challenging thing we do on earth is love and all of heaven wants to help you do that well.

A well-ordered inside

We are complex beings. Each one of us is comprised of a body, soul (including thoughts and feelings) and our will or spirit as pictured here (Figure 5.1):

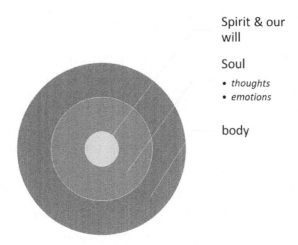

Figure 5.1 (Body, soul, and spirit)

When we are distressed, we scatter. Our bodies get revved up for fight or flight. Our thoughts race. Our emotions run wild. Our will scrambles toward anything that looks like survival or relief. You can picture a scattered moment like this (Figure 5.2):

Figure 5.2 (When we feel scattered)

In these moments we often say to ourselves "pull yourself together!" That is exactly what we need to do! We can know that- but not be able to do that. We need God's help. There are many passages that urge us to lean on the Lord's help during distressed times, but few do it so clearly as the loved Psalm 23, "The LORD is my shepherd; I shall not want. He makes me lie down in green pastures. He leads me beside still waters. He restores my soul" (Psalm 23:1-3). Notice the path back to a settled or restored soul? The Lord guides us. He first makes you lie down in green pastures. A picture of resting securely in His presence. The Lord knows what you need. He will "lead you to still waters". As we trust Him to guide, we experience a settling and gathering of ourselves. He's restoring our soul bringing a settling to our souls and peace that guards our hearts (see Figure 5.3):

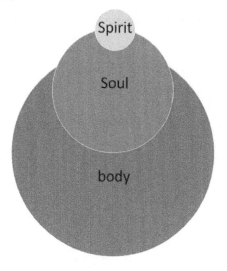

Figure 5.3 (A well-ordered soul)

God's Spirit quiets our racing emotions and stills our mind and body so we can do better work (Figure 5.3). This is not a corporate takeover by the Holy Spirit, but rather an experience like the 3-legged races we see at picnics. It is us choosing to be yoked to His guidance. We let the Shepherd guide. At first it feels clumsy, awkward, and unachievable; but Jesus' promise reminds us that, "I will ask the Father, and he will give you another advocate to help you" (John 14:16).

These thoughts give new weight and relevance to Jesus saying, "My command is this: Love each other as I have loved you" (John 15:12). And to Paul's point that, "The only thing that counts is faith expressing itself through love" (Galatians 5:6b). The Scripture is calling us to partner with God in our quest to love. It is not a singular act. It doesn't just depend on my limited ability or resources. I have available to me the very help of God.

QUESTIONS:

- How do you know your soul is scattered? (It's important to know what evidences are clearest to you when distressed)
- How do you know your soul is settled? (Additionally, it's important to know what your settled soul feels like. If you know what it feels like when settled, you can find it more easily when unsettled)

The joy of the Lord is our strength

"Mark we've been meeting for some time now, how come this isn't getting better?" Joan asked. "Fair question Joan, what are you noticing?" I replied. Her husband Tom was listening. "It seems like we are fighting even more, maybe not more; but there's a different intensity now. Does that make sense?" I answered, "Yes it does. There are a lot of factors that play into this dynamic. One common reason you're feeling this strain is that you are re-engaging. That feels intense. Re-crafting your love is challenging work. It is always worth it, but it takes us to places that definitely feel intense."

Joan and Tom have been married 12 years. Their struggles emerged almost immediately after getting married. In 1965 psychologist Bruce Tuckman introduced a model for small group development.[1] It looked like this (Figure 5.4):

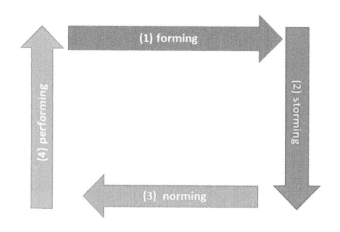

Figure 5.4 (Tuckman's stages of group development)

Tuckman had noticed that groups pass through these stages regularly. First, you form. Forming is wonderful! You have high hopes, big dreams, and some expectations for this new marriage. In the movie Bambi, you would be described by wise owl as "twitterpated". Chemically your pheromones have neutralized your rational reasoning. This happens all the time. It's understandable. Your hopes and dreams have to do with you. Then you add the other person, who has some uniquely different hopes and dreams. That leads to stage 2, storming.

We don't expect a storm to come now. It seems so early in the game. But it does. It must. If the two of you are going to happily exist in one marriage, the work must happen. It can be those little things like putting the toilet paper roll on "properly", or how you squeeze the toothpaste. Or it can be bigger issues. Issues like: you work too much or, stop looking at other women, or you can't spend like that. This is a critical turn in your marriage. If you remain stuck in storming it looks like this (Figure 5.5):

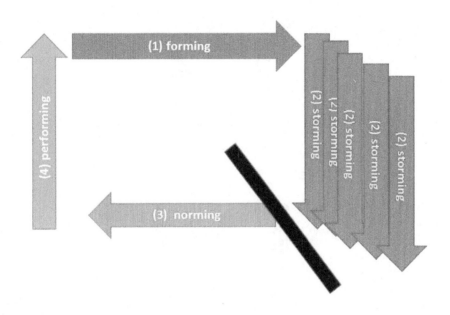

Figure 5.5 (Stuck in storming)

These repeated storms with no healthy resolution result in a growing distance between the two of you. You naturally retreat into the world of "me" because that's what feels safe to you. Now you don't see each other; you just see and feel the wall between you (Figure 5.6). It feels unscalable, undoable and irreconcilable.

64

1

2

3

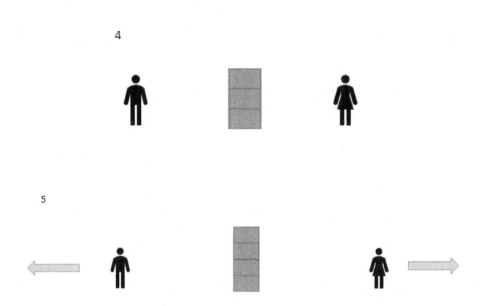

Figure 5.6 (Relational barriers because of unsuccessful storming)

The growing distance between you can be a cold, quiet space, or war zone. Both are equally dangerous. They don't foster connection, they encourage distance. That distance is what brought Joan and Tom into my office. It took 12 years, but they are risking the work now. Yes, it would have been much easier to address that initial block of conflict during year one. But here we are. And yes, that will feel intense. Don't be surprised by that if you've delayed getting help. So that was my initial answer to Joan's question regarding the intensity of what they were experiencing. I went on to say to them, "There is something you can practice that will help you both as individuals and as a couple." I asked them if they would describe themselves as "joyful". "The only thing we agree on is we are both miserable" lamented Tom. "I can understand that Tom, it's been a long arduous trip." I responded. "I'm going to say something to you that will likely make you want to punch me in the nose, but here goes..." They smiled for the first time in a long time. "Your happiness, your joy, is not dependent on your spouse. There I said it...are you with me?" I checked. "No, I'm not sure what you mean" Joan offered. Here is what I mean when I say your joy is not dependent on your spouse.

We often hear that the "joy of the Lord" is our strength. It comes from an Old Testament story in the book of Nehemiah. Nehemiah was the remarkable leader who teamed with a priest named Ezra. Together they helped the people rebuild the important wall. After working incredibly long and hard, the priest Ezra reads them God's word. They were rocked by it. After hearing it the people were distraught over the error of their ways. So much so, they began to weep. Amid this Nehemiah speaks these important words, "Do not grieve, for the joy of the Lord is your strength." (Nehemiah 8:10)

There are a few things that need to be said here. First, joy is not the same thing as 'happiness'. Happiness is based on happenings. If good things happen, then we're happy. If bad things happen, then we're sad. That isn't joy. Joy is a deep, sure sense that amid whatever is happening there is a God who is working on our behalf. He is our hope. He is our strength. He is our source and He is faithful. That is what Nehemiah is drawing the people's attention to. In a sense he is saying to the people, "Yes we have wandered from God's ways but that same God who helped us rebuild the wall will help us rebuild our lives."

You also see this perspective from the Apostle Paul as he writes the letter of joy (Philippines). Paul's in prison. Being locked up is not a great seedbed for joy. However, the devoted apostle demonstrates just how this joy of the Lord can be our strength. He prays with thanksgiving, remembering his friends, their work together, the goodness of God and the promise of what's to come. Is he delusional? No, he's joyful! He's remembering God's work and faithfulness from the past and that becomes his foundation for hope and joy. Paul is honest about his current situation, but his situation is not the thing that controls his life. He has learned to cultivate joy while surrounded by challenging circumstances. We must as well.

These are just two of the many depictions of what it looks like for a person to "return to joy". You see them through-out Scripture. But does this mean we should always be joyful? No. We need to process our emotions in a way that helps us learn and grow through them. The Psalmists are great examples of this. In Psalm 13 David displays a bit of his own process. He begins honestly in verse one, "How long, LORD? Will you forget me forever? How long will you hide your face from me?". I'd say that's pretty honest. David's not pretending. There are no rose-colored glasses here. Instead he calls out to God from where he is. Look at verse two: "How long must I wrestle with my thoughts and day after day have sorrow in my heart?" The Psalmist identifies the sorrow in his heart.

Dr. Robert Plutchik identified 8 basic human emotions in his research.[2] Plutchik's "wheel of emotion" displays how joy, sadness, fear, disgust, surprise, anticipation, anger, and trust are foundational to our other emotions. These primary emotions are also essential to our navigating life's challenges, changes, and threats. When one of them fires so does our nervous system and fight or flight responses. I've adapted Plutchik's model into my own "wheel of emotion" with joy as it's center. It looks like this (Figure 5.7):

Figure 5.7 (My adapted Plutchik wheel of emotion)

You'll notice a red line stemming from joy to anger. This depicts when we move from experiencing joy to anger. When that happens you, in a sense, slide down into a valley of anger. Which could be portrayed as this (Figure 5.8):

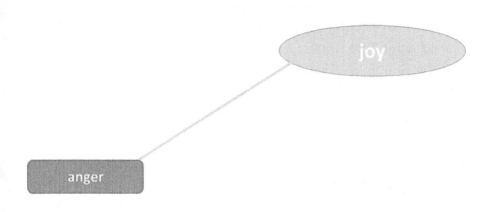

Figure 5.8 (Sliding off the center of joy)

You and I are not designed to "live from anger". We probably all know someone who does, and it is not good for them or us. What happened to that individual is they lost their way back to joy. Most of their encounters in life are colored by anger. It has become their go-to emotion and the place they work from.

Returning to David's Psalm 13 we see he has slid off into sadness. Now as he engages God from that place of sadness he is beginning to work back to joy. We know from David's story in Scripture he used a variety of tools to accomplish this. He would write poems and songs (journaling is a huge help to many), he'd sing (worship is a dynamic pathway to reconnect with joy), he'd remember (Psalmists often recall who God is or what He's done). In this Psalm David concludes with two of these practices: singing and remembering. "I will sing the LORD's praise, for he has been good to me." (Psalm 13:6)

All of this demonstrates the need for us to acknowledge our various emotions, but then work back to a center of joy. If David had remained stuck in sadness, he would have been a very different kind of King-his perspective skewed, his soul heavy and his relationships suffering greatly. David would have been an "Eyeore-like" ruler.

Joan and Tom were stuck. As Tom put it, "The only thing we agree on is we're both miserable". Misery had gripped them. Instead of seeing their partner through the eyes of joy, they could only see them as the source of their misery. I see this often in marital struggles. Each person has made their spouse into a monster. All they see, all they focus on are the negative attributes of their spouse. They've lost perspective because they've slid from joy. It's not that you want to ignore things that may need to change, but how you see them will greatly affect how you address them. That's where we need the joy of the Lord to be our strength. So, we need to get back to joy as our center. We do that by engaging our faith. It is a deeply personalized way, much like we see in the Psalms. However, there are several key stages we all pass through to get back to joy. That journey is marked by these steps (Figure 5.9):

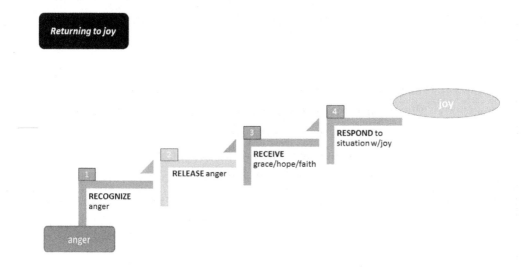

Figure 5.9 (Steps to returning to joy)

First *recognize* what's happening. Proverbs 16:2 says, "All a person's ways seem pure to them, but motives are weighed by the LORD." God wants us to see what is moving us. The driving force. If we are working towards love; love must be the motivator. Anger won't get us there. Sadness won't make it. We are designed to be fueled by joy. It must be the place we work from. When we recognize what we are feeling we can start working to release it. When John came to see me, he was very frustrated. Plopping down in the chair he confessed, "I want to scream. Just scream! Don't you get it? We don't have that kind of money!" John's wife Mary had struggled with over-spending in the past. It would get better and then occasionally slide into another spending spree.

It's challenging for us to stay close to our partners while we wait for this kind of thing to change. We tend to think "Sure I have my faults, but mine are just smaller." Smile. They are not smaller; they are just more familiar. What our partners need most from us in seasons of change is not frustration or rejection, but encouragement, assurance, and support. It's when the analogy of marriage being a dance just won't do. No, in times like this, marriage is a three-legged race!

I listened to John some more. We processed his frustration. It came down to fear. I remember seeing him recognize it. He shook his head and looked at me surprised. "Wow! I am afraid. Afraid we'll lose everything, just go completely broke." "Is the Lord showing you anything about that?" I asked. He paused, "Well not so much showing me, but I have a better sense of God's with me. I don't have to be afraid." John had found a way to *release* his anger (stage 2) and *receive* grace (stage 3).

We talked about Mary's struggle: what she may need from him and how God might have him work from this new place of fearlessness. John went home and had a different conversation with Mary. In the past they would argue to no resolve. Mary would slide into shame. Their relationship would be crippled for weeks. This time, with no fear and a hearty dose of joy they landed in much different place (stage 4-*respond*). Mary was able to discover some of what drove her overspending. Together, as a team they devised a strategy that would help her. It was the last major episode for Mary. Since then she's had a few temptations but been able to move past them. I asked her, "What changed?" "John got in it with me. I felt like he climbed right into my mess. No judgement, just there to help. I've never experienced anything like that before. It was a game-changer."

John and Mary did their work. They climbed back to joy. They worked together in concert with God's grace. Is it always presto-chango that easy? No not always, but you'll be surprised how different working from joy can be.

Earlier I mentioned Peter's exhortation in 1 Peter 5:7. It is a succinct teaching on what we need to experience in our conversations with God. Peter tells us to first cast those cares to Him. He's the One who will daily bear your burdens (Ps. 68:19). Most people practice this. We'll tell God what's bugging us. It's Peter's second step that is critical. When he says, "for God cares for you", it's not a distant, far off feeling. No, what Peter is writing about is a settled sense deep within us that says, "God's got this. He cares about my situation and He's working on it right now." Whatever is happening might not have changed, but your soul is settled. God has it. It's going to be ok. That settled sense is working from joy.

All of this puts a premium on our relationship with God. If faith is the foundation for healthy love (see Galatians 5:6b), then we must pay attention to our God's guidance. John Ortberg says it this way, "You must arrange your days so that you are experiencing deep contentment, joy and confidence in your everyday life with God."[3] (2014 "Soul Keeping Study Guide: Caring for the Most Important Part of You", p.54, Harper Collins). Crafting such a day can be greatly assisted by noting your sacred pathways (Gary Thomas) and places of renewal. These and additional helps are included in the appendix of this book.

Gaining this settled safe place within you is essential to loving well. As we learn to abide in Christ and trust His guidance, we become more confident in God's care for us. An inner safe place is developed. We have a settled sense that "God is with us". This greatly assists us in building a mutually safe place as a couple in moments when you wonder, "if I love them like that who will love me?" The answer you need is discovered through His presence, care, and grace. Your inner safe place. Because of how He loves you in the moment you can gracefully give love to another (see John 15:12).

QUESTIONS:

- Do you have some 'return to joy' experiences?
- As you read, what is the Lord emphasizing to you?
- You are about to move to creating a safe place for you and your spouse. What are you hoping for? What do you think they are looking for? Take a moment to offer that to God. Wait...for His care. You'll need a clear sense of what each of you desire as you move ahead.

Chapter 4: Creating A Safe Place For Both Of You

What's safe for me may not be safe to you

"Where are you going now?" asked Lisa. "Why do you need to know everything I'm doing all the time" retorted Tom. "Well because the Millers are coming over in 15 minutes. If you'd pay attention to me occasionally you might have remembered that."

What do you hear in that brief conversation? Defensiveness? Jabbing? Sarcasm? Is it a safe place if we're on the defensive or if we feel the need to jab? Is sarcasm fostering connection or distance? Are either Tom or Lisa operating out of their settled self? No. Let's be honest, there are times when at the speed of life, we lose track of all kinds of things. Our schedule. Our tone of voice. Our choice of words. Our marital vows! When working to build a safe place as a couple, one of the best practices you can institute is a communication time. It is not a cure-all, but it can seriously reduce the times when a conversation like Lisa and Tom's happens to you.
Communication Time

A communication time is not a date night. It is a regularly scheduled weekly time where you and your mate can sit down and discuss a number of significant areas of your marriage:

1. Your finances. Do you have any unexpected expenses coming up?

2. Your time. How is the pace of your life? Is there anything you need to schedule?
3. Your children. If you have children, you may want to discuss any concerns or news you have.
4. Your souls. How are each of you doing with life?
5. Your walk. What is the Lord teaching you? Any prayer requests?
6. Is there anything you've been waiting to tell me or ask me?

A communication time can take anywhere from hour to an hour and a half. Plan for a time when you have good energy and focus. I am married to an extrovert. For some reason we chose Sunday nights to have our communication time. That seems insane because I am a pastor. All Sunday morning, I am talking with people and preaching. I'm an introvert, so you'd think by Sunday night I'd be toast. But here's the genius of it. Because our communication time was coming that evening, I had a clear inner sense of where my energy tank was on Sunday morning. I could tell when I was about ¼ tank and I'd back off the conversations because I knew Betsy was looking forward to talking later that night. It helped me pace and prepare for our communication time. I knew Betsy would be asking me about the kids or money or something important. Having prepared, I was ready as an introvert to engage those things. It limited those moments when I'd be heading out the door just when we were supposed to be getting ready for the Millers to drop by.

QUESTIONS:

- Do you currently have something like a communication time? If so, how is it going? Does it lead to resolution or conflict? If conflicted, is there one area that you are struggling with? If that is on-going consider getting some coaching.

- If you are don't have a communication time, how do you feel about the idea? Reticent? Excited? "Oh boy another thing I have to do!?" Remember to do your best to work from joy.

Watch your rhythms of life

Having a communication time is helpful in preparing for your week together. It sets a nice rhythm of expectations. Rhythm is important to relationships. Each day, we part ways and have our various experiences. Some head off to work. Others may be at home with 3 little kids. Still others may be volunteering in some ways. But generally, couples will find their individual involvements unique to themselves and not a shared experience. This also means that your experience in life that day may be vastly different. Your boss may have been less than kind. Your kid may have thrown up all over the living room. Your car may have broken down on the highway. That means when you meet again, time may have taken you through totally different experiences. Which means you have some catching up to do!

Dan has begun a new ministry job. He's in his mid-thirties, been married 10 years and has 3 young children (ages 5, 3 and 1). Dan's wife Beth stays home with those little ones. Life is extremely busy for both of them! They come to see me.

"I don't think I can keep doing this" Beth confided. "I chase kids all day long and I'm starving for some kind of adult conversation. But when Dan comes home, he's all talked out. Where is my time?" "I'm trying, Beth," Dan responded. "I'm doing the best I can." They looked overwhelmed. "Ok you two let's think this through" I answered. "I'm going to ask you about something that is going to seem insignificant at first but humor me, ok?" "Yes" they answered. "First of all, are you having a regular communication time?" "Not always. Sometimes we are scrambling to talk about money or time. It's really hard to find a place where we both have energy." "I get it" I said. "Keep working at a good time and then prioritize the time you have to talk to hit what matters most. You can check in with each other right at the start and ask, "What do we need to talk about most tonight?" Beth and Dan nodded yes. "Now here's what is going to seem insignificant at first." "Fire away" Dan replied. "Each morning when you leave, Dan, how do you leave?" "What do you mean?" he asked. "Like what time do I go...or what?" I responded, "No, it's important to think about how you leave. It's vital to seize that moment. To hug each kid. To kiss Beth. Maybe take a moment to pray for them. Make it as positive as possible. Because that's their last memory of you. Being intentional about it can have an important influence on the day for everyone. Then as you return, asking yourself, "Are you ready to engage with them in the way you want to?"

This is not some little house on the prairie idea. Drs. John and Julie Gottman have been studying 'highly satisfied couples' for decades. Their research is extremely helpful and promising. They recently found that "rituals of connection" provide high value to couples.[1] Two of these rituals involve the coming and going of our average day. The Gottman's noted that happy couples try to learn one thing that is happening in their partner's life that day before saying goodbye in the morning. This could be lunch plans, a doctor's appointment, or a scheduled call with their parents. The goal is to ask questions and learn about the exciting and not so exciting things about your partner's day. This takes a whopping two minutes per day but provides a positive and lasting connection to your mate. Reunions are when you see your partner again at the end of the day. They encourage couples to share a hug and kiss that lasts at least six seconds. Dr. Gottman calls this a "kiss with potential."[2] The six-second kiss is a ritual of connection that is worth coming home to. I've modified this tip and called it "kiss and tell." After the six-second kiss, it's good to have a check in conversation for about 20 minutes. This provides you with a space for empathy and non-sexual intimacy, as well as encourages you to understand the stresses and problems you're both facing outside of your relationship.

Dan began to focus on his connection rituals. On days he'd have an early appointment, he'd leave a note on the counter for Beth and the kids. He took to the idea of a 6 second kiss on returning like a duck to water! During the day he'd occasionally send Beth a text letting her know that he was thinking of her. She'd often return the text with a video of something fun from the day. These simple rituals helped connect them and eased the transitional challenge of the day. So much so that child number four was on the way!

QUESTIONS:

- Do you have satisfying ways that you exit and return in your relationship?
- Anything you'd like to see different?
- One of the keys is to have mutually satisfying exits and returns as well as a measure of predictability. The predictability helps you and your partner pace your reconnection. In your communication time, talk about your rhythms noting any tweaks you want to make.

Turning towards

The idea of rhythms, leaving and joining, usually surprises couples. They don't necessarily think it would be significant until they rework theirs. There is another piece of our relating that is vital to connection. It's what the Gottmans refer to as, "turning towards each other's emotional bids". Dr. John Gottman conducted a study with newlyweds and then followed up with them six years later. The couples that remained married were much better at one thing —turning towards instead of away. In fact, happily married couples turned towards one another 86% of the time. Divorced couples averaged only 33% of the time.[3] That's a marked difference.

The key here is not just turning towards but recognizing each other's emotional bids. These bids are quiet calls for a spouse to offer attention, affirmation, affection, or help. Many times, they are subtle like a look, wink, or general comment. This happens because to bid is to risk. For most of us, to risk boldly and obviously seems too risky. So, we start with these slightly veiled bids, hoping our partner will notice. In a sense we are "testing the water". When your spouse reads it right, it fosters connection. When they don't, it creates distance because they feel misunderstood or ignored. It's not the bid itself; it is what the bid means. The bid means "I matter so much to you that you worked to figure me out." It is a dance of connection and we all have our ways of dancing. Your mission is to discover how they are stepping.

QUESTIONS:

- Do you recognize when you are extending an emotional bid to your partner? Do they usually catch it?
- How are you doing with responding to their bids?
- Responding to emotional bids really is like dancing. You have to learn the "moves" and practice. What do you need to keep dancing?

Capture moments:

A good friend asked me, "Mark how does this bidding fit with learning to ask for what you need?" Excellent question. Bids are asking. Yes, they're not as clear as a billboard sign, but it is a sign. Part of what connected you in the beginning of your relationship was something that would sound like, "they get me." What continues to hold you together is an on-going practice of getting better at getting each other. When we keep practicing with each other we are fostering trust, understanding, kindness and love.

This can sound so obscure. Maybe downright frustrating. Yet it is not as challenging as one may think. As I mentioned it's very likely that you were excellent during courtship. But life happens. I was talking to a young couple who just had their third child. The third child usually comes right when both parents are working and progressing in their careers. So that means more time, energy and focus is required of you at work, but with a third child at home that takes more time, energy and focus too. The first two kids don't just entertain themselves and somewhere in the middle of little house on the freeway you are supposed to discern the hidden meaning of a smirk from your spouse? That's pretty much what Brian said to me that day. "Mark we just don't have time or space for us as a couple, or for me as an individual. It feels like we are drowning in kids." "Yes, it's a remarkably busy season. Each season has it's learning." I tried to console. "For Laura and I we feel the drift. She gets frustrated with me if I don't pick up on what she needs. You talk about catching those bids, but I'm not getting it." I paused and answered, "It's important, Brian, but your connection as a couple is a hearty mix of things."

Continuing, I told him, "You can catch a bid, or you can capture a moment. If you catch the bid, good for you. However, if you miss it, you can still capture a moment. This involves pausing with focus. Capturing a moment happens when you pause and notice the kids playing nicely together. That focused moment is a bond for you two. When you sit down to eat a meal together and taste her freshly baked bread, pause and thank her and tell her what you like so much about her bread. You are capturing the moment. When we do that, we are soaking in the joy together. That connects us. Those are the moments that hold us together as well."

I went on to tell him about some sage advice I received from one of my graduate professors. Dr. Kassera was a bright guy. We were talking about my launching into marriage and family counseling. At 30 years old what did I know? He nodded and paused to think. His advice was short and to the point, "Well...just go slow and act stupid." "What in the world does that mean?" I countered. Dr. Kassera explained, "What most couples need is in there somewhere, and they are just racing by it. You must get them to slow down to understand. You must ask questions that help them get there. You have to go slow and act stupid." I wasn't entirely sure I got it then, but time has shown me going slow and listening is helpful. Just a quick glance at the Proverbs and you find similar advice:

Proverbs 18:2- Fools find no pleasure in understanding but delight in airing their own opinions.

Proverbs 29:20- Do you see someone who speaks in haste? There is more hope for a fool than for them.

That is just two of the numerous proverbs. See a pattern? It has to do with not slowing down enough to understand. Learning to go slow, pausing to gain understanding. That's what Dr. Kassera called "acting stupid." However, here is Solomon, one of the wisest men in history, telling us the same thing. Therefore, go slow, look for bids, catch moments, and seek understanding. Then you'll be wise, very wise and connected!

The art of going slow and acting stupid.

This advice of "going slow" and easing into hard conversations is wise. Most arguments have to do with the 'me' not the "we". It is the anxious "I". It may be your perspective or your wishes, but the majority of arguments are an; "I" versus "I". Therefore, James says plainly, "What causes fights and quarrels among you? Don't they come from your desires that battle within you?" (James 4:1). That's a proverbial 2x4 between the eyes, isn't it?

To work for the "we", a person needs clarity and understanding. That means considering with patience and kindness what my partner needs without losing hold of what I am wanting. That understanding requires time, good listening and waiting for each person to share what's on their mind. We must proceed slowly, because "meaning-making" takes time and concentration. We can easily race to incorrect meaning sending an already challenging conversation sideways with inaccuracies, accusations, and defensiveness. Every marriage represents the merger of two different tribes with different relational styles and languages. Each tribe has a wide variety of ways in which to communicate something. To understand all these dynamics, we need a high measure of calm so we can get to a solid shared meaning. Every marriage has a story about learning what that "look" really means. It might mean "don't you dare" or "let's get going", but at some point you had to have learned what it meant. All of this takes time and practice.

Therefore, Paul begins his celebrated thoughts on love with, "love is patient..." (1 Corinthians 13:4). While it is not the exclusive solution to arguments, patience is a foundational piece. Good lovers must learn how to "put themselves on hold" while they wait to understand what their mate is saying.

Larry sat up straight. His eyes glared over at his wife and then flashed towards me, "She never sees it my way..." "Never?" I asked. "That's right...NEVER!" Larry insisted. Ann, Larry's wife, was much more calculated in her assessment, "Larry always uses his temper to control me...when he loses control, he yells; just like now". Never. My way. Always. Control. That's an example of what we are talking about in this section. Neither Larry nor Ann are arguing for the "we". They've lost their way. How does that happen so quickly?

The power of calm

If you look on Amazon or go to a bookstore and peruse the shelfs for marriage books you will inevitably find most of them talk about communication and conflict resolution. To be sure those elements are vital to a healthy relationship, however neither one is possible if we lose calm. Our bodies are designed for survival. When threatened, our physiology leaps into high gear alerting our nervous system and body to prepare for fight or flight. In the meantime, our mental resources begin to shift to a reactionary mode. When trying to resolve conflicts we do not want reactionary mode! We want to respond...calmly. But if our mind is racing, or our body is stressed; neither our body nor brain will respond well. We need to quiet ourselves allowing our body to signal to our brain 'all is well'.

One of the primary tools I use is body awareness. Our bodies are like the dashboard of our souls. When we are anxious on the inside, our bodies typically will manifest some outside responses. When we are afraid internally, our bodies register that externally. Learning to note where your body registers such stress is critical. Some people will feel their jaws tighten. Others will feel their stomach knot up. Still others may feel their shoulders rise. Most everyone will hold their breath or take short, minimal breaths. What is important is your awareness of these tension signs because if you don't do some immediate calming, you are likely to react rather than respond. If you note the places of tension and intentionally relax them your body will begin to gear down. It is also important to take some deep, relaxed breaths signaling to your body and brain "hey, we're ok here."

"I can't believe I said that..." lamented Joe. "I mean I don't really mean it but in the heat of our argument I said some incredibly mean things." I nodded. I understand. Really, I do. When our bodies get tense our brains shut down. We can say some incredibly mean things when our brains shut down. "Joe describe for me what was going on in your body during this disagreement.' I queried. He looked at me perplexed. "I mean where was the tension in your body? What was happening with your breathing and your heart rate?" He looked blankly at me answering 'I don't know, I was just angry. Maybe tense. I guess I don't know"

Remember that picture of a scattered person. Their body over on one side while their thoughts, feelings and will are splattered everywhere else. That was Joe in this moment. He had no real sense of what was going on in his body. He was scattered. He was in full fight or flight.

"Have you been able to repair the damage, Joe?" "No, Cindi won't talk to me until I promise her that I'll get help with my anger. She is scared." "Joe, we either handle our anger or our anger will handle us. Do you know how to calm yourself?"

Joe and I spent a few sessions talking about where the tension begins and how to slow it down. We also talked about anger as a secondary emotion. There is almost always a bigger emotion under anger. For Joe it was being wrong and if he was wrong then he was stupid and if he was stupid then he was useless and if he was useless then he was rejected. He feared rejection. All humans do. It's one of our greatest fears. When Joe saw how his angry reactions accelerated rejection for both of them, he made a heroic effort to learn how to work from calm. That's vital because marriage offers significant challenges for all of us and calm is the ideal approach to navigating them.

QUESTIONS:

- When you are tense or angry do you know where the tension grips your body? (things like: tense jaw, shoulders go up, or stomach in knots). If you don't, it's important to begin to take note. In order to slow down and settle you need to deactivate those areas. You can only do that if you are aware of them.

- Pay attention to how you breath in challenging moments. Do you tend to hold your breath? Do you take short, shallow breaths? Relaxed easy breathing is essential to quieting down.

Chapter 5: Common Challenges

Opposites attract, or do they?

"Then the LORD God said, "It is not good that the man should be alone; I will make him a helper fit for him." (Genesis 2:18)

It began here. God recognizes Adam needs someone. It's interesting to me that Adam doesn't see that. God does. There are two key Hebrew words to note in this verse:

Helper: The Hebrew word 'Ezer'. Generally, this word is defined 'helper".

Fit: 'Neged' which typically translates as 'counterpart, suitable or opposite'

Up until now, everything God created was 'good'. He would finish a stage of creation, step back, examine His work and announce, "It is good". It's like the builder of a house. First, the foundation is built. He walks around making sure it is square and to specification then he announces, "It's good...ready for stage two." In similar fashion, the Creator is studying Adam and notes that 'it is not good' he's alone. Something is missing! God discerns that Adam needs a helper. Someone who will be a suitable counterpart. Part of that plan involves this element of an 'opposite' expressed in the Hebrew word 'neged'. Adam doesn't need more of what he has, he needs a suitable counterpart. And here is where the fun begins.

So, it appears that from the onset God allows for what we say, "opposites attract." It's not that partners need to be complete opposites. In fact, there is decent research that says people will look for a mate who shares their values, views, and perspectives. However, there is also an element of attraction where we are 'shopping' for something we need. Something that "completes us". A racer looks for a pacer. A spender is drawn to a saver. Disorganized may drift towards organized. It's not perfect science. However, in every relationship I've worked with there are places where that couple holds opposite gifts or talents or approaches to life. In most cases that can be a blessing but at times it seems to feel like a curse.

QUESTIONS:

- How are you and your spouse 'complementing' (in this Genesis sense) each other?
- Take a moment and ask God to help you see your spouse like He sees them.

Stop borrowing and start sharing

I began our pre-marriage session by asking, "So Mike what is it that you like about Lindsey?" "Everything" he quickly answered shifting even closer to her. "Everything. Ok, but can you be more specific with me?" I continued. "Well, I'm not the most organized person in the world' Mike glanced over to Lindsey to check her response. She smiled. "But Lindsey is super organized, and I love how she organizes me." I paused, looking to see how those words landed with Lindsey. She nodded. "So, do you two see a downside to that at all?" I quizzed. "No probably not. I mean I do like to organize, and Mike seems to appreciate it. So, it works." Lindsey offered.

What do you think? See any problems? Mike and Lindsey did marry and about 6 months later they were back in my office. "I can't stand it." Mike groaned. "There isn't anything that Lindsey leaves alone. She organizes my dresser drawers, our closet, our kitchen and now she's been moving things around in the garage! Isn't there anywhere I say where what goes?" I responded, "Good question...is there anywhere?" "But that wasn't what we agreed on. He told me he loved how I organized things. I'm just trying to use my gifts." Lindsey explained.

See the challenge? It's not always this clear, but here's what I've observed. Often, we begin a relationship with "borrowing" the other's talent, but after time we must learn to 'share' in whatever the other has lent us. For example, I like to shop. Especially for my latest passions. Back when I raced bikes, I would build persuasive arguments for why I needed a new one. Compelling things like, "You want me to be safe right?" Betsy, who is thrifty, would have to forfeit my physical safety or acquiesce to my spending frenzy. At one point she shared with me, "I feel like I am Mrs. No. I'm the one who has to put the kibosh on your latest purchasing pursuit." That did it. I got it. No fun to be that. We talked about a better process for sharing in our purchases. It took work. We shared our perspectives. We asked for counsel. We prayed. We compromised. I struggled with flare ups, especially after those glossy catalogues arrived in the mail. However, I did not want Betsy to be Mrs. NO. It's not fair if she has to be the killjoy in the spending department. We needed to re-work that dynamic in our relationship. That meant I had to stop borrowing Betsy's thrifty ability and start sharing in the responsibility.

This is an important pattern to consider in your teamwork. One sure litmus test is if your spouse feels frustrated like Betsy did. It's the weight of their over-work matched with our under-work. Be watchful as you work to discover what "sharing" might look like. Often, we can try and mimic our spouse's style. Like if I just stop spending all together. An extreme shift to the other side. To land in the healthiest place of "sharing" means that both perspectives are represented in your compromise. In our situation, Betsy had a strong propensity not to spend. She rarely bought things for herself. As we worked to compromise, she needed a dose of spending.

Working towards these compromises requires honesty and maturity. At times we need to defer to our partner's perspective because it suits the situation best. Ultimately, we want to be asking God for wisdom (see James 1:5) because wisdom helps us see life through God's eyes. He sees what the problem is and wants to help us. Our faith in Him and partnership together can best resolve it. In that sense, problems can be seen as "heaven-sent" provocations calling us to bring our struggles to a Loving God who longs to help us! Blaming someone doesn't solve the problem. That just fixes the blame on one person, causing more division and shame. Furthermore, we cannot afford to allow problems to stay between us and create a barrier. What we need to do is place the problem in front of us, stand side by side and ask God what to do about it. It isn't up to us to solve it; it is up to us to bring it to God!

This simple but difficult "discipline" has been a constant help to Betsy and me. There have been times when we have written down the problem on a piece of paper and physically set it in front of us as we stood side by side and prayed for help.

This first picture depicts when a challenge hits couples and they can't immediately see a solution. It tends to *feel like* something is between us (Figure 6.0).

Figure 6.0 (A problem between us)

In the tension of these moments it's easy to slide into fixing blame instead of fixing the problem. Looking at a newly opened bill Heidi laments "Greg are you kidding me? The car cost almost $1800 to fix? What?!" "I guess so Heidi...you told me to get it fixed so I did. That's what it cost." "Yeah but within reason. 1800 bucks is a lot of money." The conversation continued in my office. "So, what are the two of you going to do?" I asked. "I don't know. We don't have 1800 dollars we can just throw up in the air." Tagging someone as the problem isn't the solution (Figure 6.1). They were just trading blame back and forth over whose fault it was. Heidi blamed Greg for spending $1800 dollars and Greg blamed Heidi for asking him to get it fixed.

Figure 6.1 (Tagging someone as "the problem" doesn't solve the problem)

The answer isn't found in who to blame. What they really needed to unload was the pressure of an $1800 car bill. "Can I ask you a question? What is the clearest thing God has shown you about the situation?" I queried. It slowed them down. "I'm not sure I know" offered Greg. Heidi nodded in similar fashion. "Maybe His perspective can help," I continued. Our time was coming to a close. "Tell you what. You've been passing this back and forth, like a hot potato. What if you put it in front of you, both facing it shoulder to shoulder and talk together about what God may want to do (Figure 6.2). Next week let's pick up here. If you feel it between you, don't let it stay there. The two of you are listening together for what God wants to say about it, not tagging someone with the problem. Ok?" "Got it," they announced together. We prayed. I reminded them of Psalm 68:19,

"Praise be to the Lord, to God our Savior, who daily bears our burdens" as they left.

Now I know some may think that's "pie in the sky" kind of thinking. But the reality is that love takes faith. God wants to be involved. We need to watch how He might be getting involved. The next week here's what Greg and Heidi came back with:

1. Heidi said she was "convicted about her reaction". She asked Greg to take the car in. He did it right away. But when she saw the bill, "she freaked". She apologized to Greg saying, "I reacted...I didn't respond well...sorry."

2. Greg reached over and hugged Heidi. He then apologized for being defensive. "It was pretty clear to me when I thought it through and started praying, I had shut down and pulled away from you."

3. They both told me that they want to team together better. There was no budget amount set for the repair. They'd do that differently. They also talked more about how they planned their overall budget. The notion of praying together about these things came up.

This meeting had a totally different feel. No finger pointing or blame. I asked them what was different. "We didn't even think of asking God for help" Greg answered. "You found it helpful huh?" I asked. "Definitely" they responded.

I'm a realist. I know not every situation is going to wrap up nicely like a 30-minute TV show. But I meet with a lot of Christian couples who don't enlist prayer in their relationship. Most are like Greg and Heidi. They just don't think of it. Please make it a practice to pray. Especially when you feel stuck in your problem solving. Like Greg and Heidi, you can discover new perspectives, finding grace to navigate the struggle and gain wisdom for the future. That's not a bad result!

Figure 6.2 (Putting the problem in front of you)

QUESTIONS:

- When you read about Greg and Heidi's situation which person do you relate to most?
- How do you as a couple resolve these kinds of conflicts?
- What is one thing God is showing you to apply to your practice as a couple?

Life happens

I've been married for 38 years now. When we were first married, I was a marathon runner. Now I walk slowly in the woods. That was then, this is now. Life happens. The seasons of life bring change. We learn to grow and adapt. But it is change. In my work with couples I've discovered that we have to get "re-married" numerous times over the lifespan. No, I'm not suggesting you go find a new partner every time life changes. Reality is that you and your spouse are already changed. If what impacts us are our relationships and experiences in life, then we all encounter a myriad of life changing events and stages.

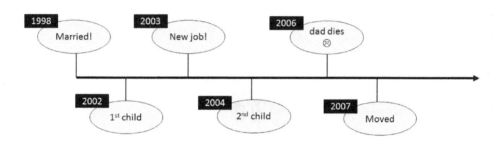

Figure 6.3 (Life events where Dan and Kristin needed to "remarry")

Dan and Kristin came into my office slowly and sat down. "We're really hoping you can help us, Mark" Kristin offers. She continued, "We used to be so happy with each other. Neither one of us knows what happened to us. We just go through the motions." Dan nodded. Then they began to tell me about all the changes that had come their way over the past 9 years (see Figure 6.3 above). Two children, one of which was born prematurely with complications. Then the loss of a dearly loved father. Shortly after his dads passing, Dan's company requested he take this new role. That meant more hours and some traveling. All these events eroded the time and energy Dan and Kristin would have available for each other.

"Tell me about how you remarried after your first child." I asked. Dan shifted in his chair, "What do you mean, remarried?" "I mean did married life change after your first child?" "Oh absolutely! Lindsey was premature and had a number of big challenges her first year" Kristin offered. "Exactly," I said. "With those changes, we change. The space we relate in changes and we have to figure out what it will look like to be happily married in this new season." "Ugh we are barely keeping our noses above it all, Mark," Dan groaned. "All the more important then Dan. It usually isn't like reinventing the wheel, but it takes some thinking and conversations. Otherwise you find yourself just going through the motions. By the way, this is why a weekly communication time is so helpful. You can take care of these changes in bite-sized chunks," I coached.

Here's what I shared with them:

1. **Acknowledge the change and the significance**. Most of us with children would acknowledge that the first one was a game-changer. Simple things like, what restaurant you'd like to eat at turn into fog-filled sleepless debates about who is going to get up now?

2. **Notice what is different and how you are responding to it**. Dan and Kristin knew something had changed but were grasping at straws. When your connection changes, it's usually because the season has shifted. There can be other reasons but check the season first.

3. **Think and talk about what your best connections were and where they are now**. A large part of what maintains our connections is shared experiences: the things you enjoy doing together. For Dan and Kristin, the first child radically altered their primary connections. After Lindsey was born, they were really stretched. They dropped out of small group and volunteering and no longer could run together or work on projects as a team because they were taking shifts caring for Lindsey. So, four of their primary connections radically shifted with this one life change (Figure 6.4).

Closeness comes from sharing experiences together

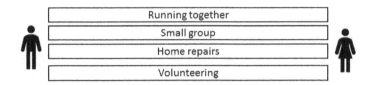

Figure 6.4 (Experiences that bonded Dan and Kristin)

For Dan and Kristin connections changed radically (lost running together, small group and volunteering), so it's understandable they feel a disconnect (Figure 6.5).

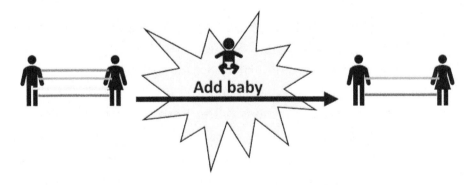

Figure 6.5 (Lost relational connections between Dan and Kristin)

4. **Be intentional about discovering new connections and maximize them.** These calls to "re-marriage" happen all through the lifespan not just to young couples like Dan and Kristin. My wife and I recently transitioned to an "empty nest". Some of those connections that were fostered through co-parenting have changed and we now have time and energy to foster new connections between us. Lately we have taken up birdwatching. It has been a joy. The days where we spot a Rose-breasted Grosbeak together binds our connection deeper and makes our bond stronger.

5. **Have a clear picture of what you are building as a couple, like a vision statement if you will.** Betsy and I didn't know much when we walked down the aisle, but we certainly agreed on three things:
    1. We wanted to learn to be the best husband and wife we could.
    2. We knew we wanted to parent well.
    3. We wanted to help the church in whatever ways we could.

    We didn't need to be rich. We didn't need to be popular. We were more like Ma and Pa Kettle...just good ole family folk. But our marriage, family and church meant the world to us then. It does now. I'm still working on being a good husband. Betsy says she has the wife thing nailed down. We'd do most anything for our 5 kids and their spouses and you'll find us serving the church with our whole heart.

QUESTIONS:

- Have you kept up with the seasons of marriage?
- How have you deliberately gotten remarried as a couple?
- How are your connections as a couple? Are there some new ones you can foster?
- Is your vision for marriage clear and agreed upon?

Chapter 6: Intimacy

When I began counseling and pastoring in the 1980's there was only one Christian book on sex I could find. It was Dr. Ed Wheat's classic entitled, "Intended for Pleasure".[1] It remains an excellent read. There just weren't many Christians talking about sex. Almost 40 years later there are more books, but I find that most couples are still not talking about it. Therefore, my aim in this chapter is not so much to give you sex tips, but rather help you talk about sex. More exactly I want to shed some light on the six thoughts below (Figure 6.7):

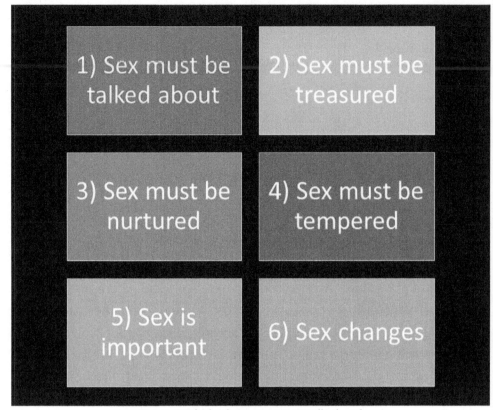

Figure 6.7 (What's important to talk about)

1. Sex must be talked about

We had met for 5 sessions and not really hit anything significant. I spoke up, "You know, we've talked about a number of things over these past sessions, but it seems like we haven't really hit why you are here. Let me ask it this way- when will you know we are done?" She looked down. He looked at her, then me and quietly said, "When we start having sex again." The room went cold. "Look you two, this counseling thing works best when we risk honesty and try to talk here about things that we can't seem to talk about anywhere else. Do you trust me?" They nodded yes.

"Well, let's try talking about this. We'll go at whatever pace you are able" I encouraged.

It was arduous but worth it. Over the next sessions we unpacked a lot of difficult history, abuse, and plenty of misunderstandings. The pain she carried was deep. She struggled to find words regarding what she was feeling. "Mostly, I feel like a big disappointment to him," she summed up with tears running down her face. Feeling like a disappointment isn't the least bit sexy for anyone. Her husband didn't know most of this. He just knew that she didn't like sex, so he stopped asking for it. They went almost 3 years before they came to see me. That's a long time.

Sex is important to a marriage. Marriage is where we are to enjoy this rapturous delight of intimacy. It creates deep bonds in our bodies and brains. It is a gift from God. He intends for it to be a pleasure charge celebration of your relationship. But a big part of getting to that connection is talking about sex OUTSIDE THE BEDROOM.

Jim and Conni are a fun young couple. They've been married for 5 years now and a have a two-year-old son. As they came into the office, Conni didn't hesitate, "Jim didn't want to come in, but I don't know what to do. I really love Jim. But we are having some problems." I studied both of them. They looked tense and confused. I offered, "Well it's probably good for us to talk then. Jim as we get started anything you want to say?" "I'm going to cut to the chase...is that ok?" "Absolutely," I affirmed. "It's seems pretty weird to have to go talk to someone about something so personal, something so natural as sex," Jim sighed. "I can appreciate that Jim. Can I ask you something?" "Yes," Jim replied. "Is sex important to you?" I queried. Looking a bit embarrassed, Jim was now studying me, searching to see if I was baiting him. I wasn't. "Ah yes. Isn't it important to every couple?" he offered. "Yes, it is. I'd say very important. So important that if for some reason a couple wasn't happy with their intimacy then it would make a little sense to find someone to process that with you. Reality is, Jim, that just about every couple I see will at some time ask a question about sex." Jim leaned into the conversation, "Really?" "Really" I continued. "It's important that we pace well here you two. When we talk about challenging topics, we tend to want to race through it because it feels uncomfortable to us. While understandable, that's not ideal. To make the best sense of things we have to understand them well. That takes time. So, breathe and do your best to relax. It appears to me that you both are hoping for your intimate relationship to get better, is that right?" They looked at one another, first affirming each other and then letting me know, "Yes."

A quick aside here. Studies indicate that couples do not go see a counselor until after 6 years.[2] I'm guessing that is 6 years after they realize something is not working. That's far too long. Jim and Conni are wise to seek help soon. Here's the advice I give myself and others. If you are stuck, ask someone you trust for perspective. Get their advice in whether or not seeking help is appropriate. Now, back to Jim and Conni.

I asked them, "What would each of you say you are struggling with?" Jim reported that Conni didn't appear interested in sex after the birth of their son. Connie's face fell. I caught that. "Can we pause for a moment?" "Yes," they answered. I just wanted to slow this down. Have you two talked about your struggles outside the bedroom?" They looked surprised. I continued, "Oftentimes these things come up as we are moving towards intimacy. Lots of hormones are flowing in our bodies. That doesn't always make for the best conversations." "That makes sense Mark, but we've never really talked about it outside the bedroom. Actually, it's kind of icy between us for days and we avoid one another," Jim informed me. "This is hard isn't it?" I affirmed. Conni looked ready to talk now. "Conni what do you think has happened?" Her eyes began to water as she mustered words, "I guess I haven't put it all together before this. I sure haven't talked with Jim or anyone. After our boy was born, I must have had some post-partum. It wasn't terrible but I was just dull. Also, my body had been through a lot during delivery. He was a big baby and it was my first. My body hasn't really been able to relax. Somehow, it's all connected. Then practically I tense up when we are going to have intercourse. Instead of being receptive it's like my body screams 'stop!' If Jim enters me, it's painful. Then my mind races into a terrible spiral of thoughts. This is wrong. I'm failing. Why doesn't this work? I'm everywhere but intimately close to Jim." I watched Jim take hold of Connie's hand. They both were discovering what was in the way of intimacy. Together we discussed next steps. Conni planned to see her gynecologist. They would talk more and gently rediscover what intimacy could look like in this season. Those steps together can become some of the greatest foreplay you could experience!

QUESTIONS:

- Do you two talk about sex outside the bedroom?
- If not, do you feel like you need to get some coaching?

2. Sex must be treasured

"Marriage should be honored by all, and the marriage bed kept pure." (Hebrews 13:4a)

If you look at most magazine racks, provocative titles and pictures are everywhere. Commercials use sexually charged jokes or images to sell their products. Pornography has far reaching impacts hitting both genders and every age. Is it possible to treasure sex? Yes, and I'd say it's more critical now than ever.

I worked in a large factory for a season. The guys there were amused that a budding pastor would join them. It became the personal mission of several them to provoke me to swear or look at a "dirty magazine". They used to call my name and hold up a magazine taunting me. One day, one of these characters sat down with me at lunch. "How come you don't look at the pictures? I mean it's ok to look right?" he asked me. I responded, "Look, I don't want to see any picture of anyone but my wife. And if you have pictures of my wife, I'll murder you!" He laughed. I continued, "Listen, can I ask you a question?" "Sure," he responded. "When you are intimate with your wife and you close your eyes, who do you see?" His face went white. It hit him. It's not his wife he's seeing. He said to me, "Ugh it's sure not my wife". "Then who are you making love with?" There was no more taunting me with pictures after that conversation. In fact, numbers of them would come around during breaks to talk about some of their marital struggles.

This is Jesus' concern when he says, *"You have heard that it was said, 'You shall not commit adultery.' But I tell you that anyone who looks at a woman lustfully has already committed adultery with her in his heart."* (Matthew 5:27-28). At first, my co-workers thought I was a strait-laced, goody two shoes kind of guy, but honestly, I want the best sex possible between Betsy and me. So, I guard it. I treasure it. No one else can have it. That isn't religious. That isn't strict. That's just plain smart.

QUESTION:

- How do you treasure intimacy in your marriage?

3. Sex must be nurtured

When you are in a growing relationship with someone it takes time to get to know them. That relationship grows as you talk and listen. You get to know their friends, about their career, dreams, and family. There's a lot to learn. If the person matters to you, then knowing them is worth the time. Sex is no different.

When I began pre-marriage counseling, I was hesitant to talk to couples about intimacy. Nowadays I insist on it. Not that I want to be intrusive, but I know how important it is to talk about it. Stu and Char are getting ready for their wedding. We've met a few times and talked about subjects they had selected as important to them. "Next time we meet I'd like to talk with you two about intimacy. Would you be OK with that?" I asked. They shuffled their feet looking down and Stu replied, "I think it's OK. Do you suspect something is wrong?" "No Stu, not at all. I have just found over the years that people generally need to find ways to talk about it, but we don't. I'd like to help lay some groundwork for you and Char. OK?"

The next meeting, I talked with them about some of these same principles I'm writing about. It was a classic example of the importance of talking about sex is. Here's a list:

1. Their expectations for the honeymoon night were vastly different. Stu anticipated several times of intercourse and Char was unsure if they'd even have the energy to have sex! Given that young couples have just been through planning and doing a wedding with all the people and pictures, Char's point is fair. In fact, newlyweds have reported back to me how glad they were that they tempered the expectations of the night. In reality it is one night and just the beginning of your sexual relationship. Granted it is an important night, but just part of a lifelong process of growing more intimate over time.

2. Stu had been sexually active prior to meeting Char who was a virgin. They had talked about this briefly but during our discussion Char confessed being worried about comparisons. That's not something you "fix" but rather acknowledge. It helped Stu communicate his care for Char as they built their sexual relationship.

3. Char had come from a family that didn't talk about sex. Her tendency was to think it was kind of dirty. Stu's education came from the locker room and magazines. So, it was critical for them to begin talking about their vision for sex. What they hoped for. What they were comfortable with and uncomfortable with.

QUESTIONS:

- Are you content with your intimate life as a couple?
- What are you thankful for? Anything you hope would be different?
- Is God placing anything on your heart that would nurture your intimacy?

4. Sex must be tempered

Numerous surveys have estimated the frequency of sexual intercourse for couples aged 30 to 50 is between 1 to 2 times per week. The average time for intercourse is estimated to be between 5 to 10 minutes.[3] That leaves a lot of time to fill! Media would have you believe that you should experience mind blowing sex multiple times per day. Not even close to reality. Reality is kids come along. That has a profound impact on your sexual activity. Our health can vacillate and affect our intimacy. Stressors like finances, work and family also influence our sexual practice.

When John, our fourth child, was about 4 months old we started to sleep decently again. Sleep is an immensely helpful thing! One night, as we were realizing our nervous systems were recovering, Betsy and I were laying side by side. She offered, "I suppose we should make love". Smiling "I said I suppose so. But I don't think I have that kind of energy." We laughed. We kissed for a bit, but reality was we were still both really tired. "We should make a date" Betsy suggested. "Absolutely!" I affirmed. So, we planned a little getaway later in the month (and saved up energy!) Our perspective regarding intimacy was being tempered. We were talking about it (yes, I realize it was in the bedroom!) and working to care for us as a couple.

When you notice that your intimacy has changed, it is critical to talk about it. Even if the answer may appear obvious-like a baby. The conversation will help you temper expectations and work to adjust to a new season. There are places in the lifespan of a marriage that naturally contribute to seasons. Here's a short list:

- Children
- Child-rearing challenges (learning & behavioral)
- Infertility
- Extended family stress (aging parents, disagreements, etc.)
- Work related stress
- Financial stress
- Health concerns (fitness, illness, addictions)
- Boredom (a very real thing!)

There are likely more, but this list is what I frequently hear from couples. They don't make sex impossible, but they do present challenges. Learn to talk about them. Better yet to talk through them to a new understanding and agreement on your sexual practice. If you are stuck, it's critical to go see someone who can help you process.

QUESTIONS:

- Were there any items on the short list above you resonated with?
- Is so, have you as a couple started talking about it?
- Is there anything you would add to the list?

5. Sex is important

They had a very refined look about them. Well dressed and composed. Sitting down, Sue pointedly started the conversation, "We disagree about sex. He thinks it's really important and I'm not that interested." Taking a breath and scrambling to mentally catch up I answered, "Thanks, Sue, I'd like to hear more about why you believe that, but right now I want to check with Bill." "It's basically true. I'd like to have sex fairly often, but Sue isn't really interested," Bill confirmed.

Think with me. If you were in my chair what would you say? Is sex that important? Should Bill just adjust? Should Sue engage even though she's 'not that interested'? There's are a lot of angles to this conversation aren't there?

I asked them if we could have the luxury of taking some time to work together, taking a comprehensive look at their life together as a couple. Married for 17 years, they now had two teenagers at home. There were some other features that stood out to me as well. Fortunately, they agreed to invest the time. Here's what we discovered:

- Sue's thyroid had been slowly declining. This had gone undiagnosed for some time. Just that alone can nullify any sexual drive.
- With Sue's thyroid problem there was accompanying depression.
- A lot of the activities they had shared (camping, hiking, biking) had gone by the wayside. Sue was too tired. The absence of these connecting activities fostered a felt distance between the two of them. Bill actually wondered if Sue was having an affair. Sue laughed at the thought saying, "Oh that would take way too much energy!"

- They had tried to talk about their intimate struggles, but it often followed Bill's rejected advances. It would have been better to find a time to talk about sex outside of the bedroom. They didn't. So that growing uncertainty about what was happening created more distance between them.

- Lastly, they were sexually active before being married. That turned out to be a struggle for Sue. She had mixed feelings about it. Sue said, "Even then there was part of me absent during sex. I didn't feel like I could give all of me." That had an obvious impact on Sue's interest and engagement sexually.

A lot there right? It wasn't just "not interested". There is always a story behind the story. During the course of our meetings, Sue asked me one time, "OK, so is sex really that important?" I smiled answering, "Yes...because sex is more than just sex. It's a singular event that impacts every part of your person and relationship. We know that intimacy positively influences your body, brain, emotions, and bond. So yes, it's important."

Sex is important. It is a gift from God. He means for it to be blessing and a source of connection for you as a couple. I'm happy to say that Sue and Bill experienced a deep renewal in their intimate life. It took some work, but it was good work.

QUESTIONS:

- Do you agree that sex is important to a marriage?
- Are there any areas you'd like to talk with your spouse about something but don't know how? Is there anyone you know who can help you process that? That conversation you're holding may be an important one.

6) Sex changes

I'm 62. That used to be old to me. Presently I consider that mid-life! But things have changed. I don't recover from exercise as quickly. I don't sleep as well. I move slower. Wouldn't it also make sense that sexually I'm adjusting as well? Absolutely. What's true for me is true for most of us. Hormonal levels drop off. Women hit menopause. Men hit something. That's what I want to zero in on.

Karen and Bill have been married 39 years and raised 4 children. Both Bill and Karen are close to retiring and they are looking forward to traveling together. Sitting down in my office they say it might be good to have this "tune-up session". We catch up talking about life changes and the family. They've done an excellent job of balancing parenting and partnering. Bill and Karen share a lot of common interests, are involved together at their church, and genuinely enjoy one another's company. So, I'm thinking to myself, "Why are we meeting?" Then Karen looked at Bill with compassion. The look appeared to hold a lot of meaning. Bill nodded to her. These moments display in living color all the work of how they respond to their emotional bids and signals. They knew each other very well. Karen took a breath and began, "I asked Bill if we could talk about our intimate life. It's been the one challenging conversation we've not done well with." Karen looked Bill's way as if to insure she was communicating this well for the both of them. After another long breath Karen continued, "Bill's interest or desire just isn't there. I'm not sure if that's me or that's normal." You could feel the anxiety rise in the room. They were holding a lot of emotion. I stepped in, "Can I say something here, you guys?" "Sure," they answered, looking a little relieved for the pause. "One of the surest things I can tell you after working with lots of couples is that sex changes. For a lot of reasons. When it does it's important to talk about it like we are today. But the fact that it has changed doesn't mean that we're broken. Or that sex is over. But it has likely changed. Together you two have figured a lot of things out. I suspect you can do fine here as well." Bill's shoulders dropped. He smiled and began to share saying, "I'm not sure for me what it is. I have battled some depression. Work has been increasingly stressful. I get done with a day and I'm shot. When I go to bed all I'm thinking about is going to sleep fast! I love Karen. I just don't have much energy." We processed quite a bit for the next 45 minutes and then did 2 follow up sessions. Here's some important things for aging couples to know:

1. **Sex changes.** Our bodies change, so it just plain makes sense. Acknowledge the changes you're experiencing. For Bill it was depression, lower energy, and high demands at work.

2. **Talk together about the changes.** There are a lot of unknowns as we age. Spaces where we are left to make meaning and that's tricky. Karen wondered if Bill found her attractive anymore. Understandable, but not the issue. They needed to talk through what these changes meant.

3. **Adapt to the changes**. I know couples that make dates on their calendar. One couple rendezvous at lunch time because they have energy then! Another couple have discovered that holding each other at night sometimes leads to sex and other times just a long comfortable good night. But they are happy. They are connected. They have adapted.

4. **Check in with each other through the changes**. Bill and Karen made some changes. Some helped; others weren't the best. But they kept changing and learning. Their intimacy deepened. Adjusting to life's seasons requires determination and patience. Yet working together builds yet another strong bond that holds you together as a couple.

5. **Don't hesitate to seek good medical advice**. In my experience, most of the challenges senior couples have sexually are related to their aging bodies. Back problems, menopause, erectile dysfunction,

vaginal dryness, fatigue, and a host of other things. Often a health professional can give you sound advice and help towards making the adaptations you may need. Do your best to resist any embarrassment and shame and visit your doctor.

There is a reason sex is often referred to as intimacy. Good sex is discovered in close intimacy. A place where each of you can freely share your thoughts and feelings and work through to a place of understanding. That mutual understanding is integral to intimacy. Frequently when your sex life is struggling it is reflective of your need to work out a new understanding. Practicing these principles can help you in that quest.

Chapter 7: The Greatest Of All Is Love

I have a good but challenging job. It often takes me into people's living rooms where they argue, or cling to addictions, or hear tough news. It also takes me to people's bedsides where they are breathing their last. When you are on the edge of life you mostly look back because it's not entirely clear what is ahead. Never in four decades of work have I heard people talk about the car they wish they'd bought, or the promotion they were passed over for. Nope. People always, and I mean always, talk about relationships. Especially close ones. They worry about how their spouse will do. They tell their kids they love them. They say the things they wish they'd said years ago but now father time is pulling their hand, so they say it. "Say what you need to say," as the singer John Mayer advises.[1]

But why is this the case? Why after 88 years of life does the person not think about their stuff but rather their people? I believe it's because "love is the greatest" (I Cor. 13:13). Love. It's what drove the Greatest (God) to perform the greatest act (give His Son) to reach the greatest number (whosever believes) with the greatest gift (eternal life) (John 3:16). Love is the greatest. It's Christ's greatest command to us in John 13:34 and it becomes the greatest sign that we are His followers in John 13:35. Love is greatest call of our life. Isn't this what Jesus makes so clear in Mark 12:28-31 NIV? "One of the teachers of the law came and heard them debating.

Noticing that Jesus had given them a good answer, he asked him, "Of all the commandments, which is the most important?" (29) "The most important one," answered Jesus, "is this: 'Hear, O Israel: The Lord our God, the Lord is one. (30) Love the Lord your God with all your heart and with all your soul and with all your mind and with all your strength.' (31) The second is this: 'Love your neighbor as yourself.' There is no commandment greater than these."

It is the greatest. There is no greater gift than for us to be loved and no greater gift than us giving love to another. While in graduate school, I conducted a random study interviewing as many people as I could find whose story demonstrated a radical shift in their ability to love. Technically their attachment style moved from being insecure to secure. Two things were resident in the 40 plus interviews I conducted. First, they had encountered in a deep and real way the love of God. Romans 8:15 as a reality for them, "The Spirit you received does not make you slaves, so that you live in fear again; rather, the Spirit you received brought about your adoption to sonship. And by him we cry, "Abba, Father." Secondly, they had a life impacting relationship with a mentor/model of love. This mentor's love provided tangible and practical experiences of what love looks like. These two features were clearly evident in their stories.

Now imagine with me. This place you and I call church. The place where Paul says, "The goal of this command is love, which comes from a pure heart and a good conscience and a sincere faith" (1 Tim. 1:5). So, in that place we devote ourselves to doing what Jesus commanded- "A new command I give you: Love one another. As I have loved you, so you must love one another (John 13:34). As we dedicate ourselves to loving and living like Jesus, the reputation of that place is marked with one distinctive- "By this everyone will know that you are my disciples, if you love one another" (John 13:35). Think about it. How different would your life be? How would your marriage look? Your family? Your community? Your workplace and schools? What would be the result of a radical, sold-out, passionate pursuit of living with this one aim- to love like Jesus? What would happen? I think you and I would agree that where we live would be a vastly different place. A better place.

That possibility all begins with you. When you determine to learn love with all your might, a significant change happens in you, your spouse, your family, your workplace, your community. Because in every one of those relationships love is invading. Love is working. Love is being practiced. And love is the greatest. Love never fails. Love remains. So, with my closing words I exhort you, love one another.

Notes

Chapter 1: Why is Love So Hard?

1. Brown, Brene. *Dare to Lead*. New York: Random House, 2018.
2. Brown, Brene. 17.
3. *Myers & Briggs Foundation*. 2020. April 2020.

Chapter 2: You Give What You Got.

1. Karen, Robert. *Becoming Attached*. New York: Oxford University Press, 1998.
2. Levine, Amir. *Attached: The New Science of Adult Attachment and How it Can Help You Find and Keep Love.* New York: Penquin Publishing Group, 2010.

Chapter 3: Jesus, The Safe Place.

1. Tuckman, Bruce W. (1965). "*Developmental Sequence in Small Groups*". Psychological Bulletin. 63 (6): 384-399.
2. Pultchick, Robert., Kellerman, Henry. *Theories of Emotion*. New York: Academic Press. 1980.

3. Ortberg, John. *Soul Keeping: Caring for the Most Important Part of You*. Grand Rapids: Zondervan, 2014.

Chapter 4: Creating a Safe Place for Both of You.
1. Gaspard, Terry. *Gottman.com/blog*. 23 July 2015. 8 July 2019.
2. Gaspard, Terry. *Gottman.com/blog*. 23 July 2015. 8 July 2019.
3. Brittle, Zach. *Gottman.com/blog*. 1 April 2019. 1 August 2019.

Chapter 6: Intimacy.
1. Wheat, Ed. *Intended for Pleasure*. Grand Rapids: Revell, 1977.
2. Gaspard, Terry. *Gottman.com/blog*. 23 July 2015. 8 July 2019.
3. Twenge, J.M., Sherman, R.A. & Wells, B.E. *"Declines in Sexual Frequency Among American Adults"*. Arch Sexual Behavior 46 (2017): 2389-2401.

Chapter 7: The Greatest of All is Love.
1. Mayer, John. *"Say"*. By John Mayer. 2007.

Bibliography

Brittle, Zach. *Gottman.com/blog*. 1 April 2015. 1 August 2019.

Brown, Brene. *Dare To Lead*. New York: Random House, 2018.

Gaspard, Terry. *Gottman Institute*. 23 July 2015. 8 July 2019.

Karen, Robert. *Becoming Attached*. New York: Oxford University Press, 1998.

Levine, Amir. *Attached: The New Science of Adult Attachment and How It Can Help You Find and Keep Love*. New York: Penquin Publishing Group, 2010.

Mayer, John. "Say." By John Mayer. 2007.

Myers Briggs Foundation. 2020. April 2020.

Ortberg, John. *Soul Keeping: Caring For the Most Important Part of You*. Grand Rapids: Zondervan, 2014.

Robert Plutchik., Henry Kellerman. *Theories of Emotion*. New York: Academic Press, 1980.

Thomas, Gary. *Sacred Pathways*. Grand Rapids: Zondervan, 1996.

Tuckman, Bruce. "Developmental Sequence in Small Groups." *Psychological Bulletin* 1965: 384-399.

Twenge, J.M., Sherman, R.A. & Wells, B.E. "Declines in Sexual Frequency Among American Adults." *Arch Sex Behavior 46* (2017): 2389-2401.

Wylie, Mary Sykes. "Mindsight." *Psychotherapy Networker Magazine* (2004): 34-37.

Helps

GENOGRAM QUESTIONS: *Please be generous to yourself with the space and pace you move through your story. If you hit some tough places consider stepping away from this for a bit and talking to someone you trust.*

PART ONE- to be completed individually

QUESTIONS ABOUT WHO WAS IN YOUR LIFE?

- Who showed you love?
  - How so?

- Who hurt you?
  - How?

- Who did you trust?
  - How come?

- Who was safe?
  - Why did they feel safe?

- Who was available to you when you had a need?

- How did you cope with challenges?

WHAT HAPPENED AROUND YOU:

- If someone from the outside watched your family do life, what would they say love meant?

- How was love shown?

- When was love given?

- When was love withheld?

- What do you wish you would have received?

- What do you wish you would have given?

PART TWO- to be completed individually

QUESTIONS ABOUT LIFE NOW

- What do you wish for now?

- What triggers you and feels like bad family?

- What feels good/safe to you?

- Where do you get stuck GIVING love?

- Where do you get stuck RECEIVING love?

- What part of your upbringing still "shadows" you?

- Where does your marriage feel like your parents?

- Who in your life now models "good love"?

- Given all this information, what do you need to learn in order to love well?
    - Who can help you with that?

PART THREE: talking about your genogram story with your spouse.

QUESTIONS FOR YOU TO DISCUSS WITH YOUR SPOUSE

- What is important for me to know about your genogram/story?

- What do we want our relationship and love to look like?

- How do we want our relationship to be remembered by family and friends?

- What is ONE thing I can do to stretch toward you?

- As we stretch, how can we encourage one another?

- What is Jesus saying to us?

Finding Help

Marriage is the most wonderful, intimate, complex, frustrating relationship on the planet. You're friends. You're often co-parents. You're lovers. You're a Christian family. All these various elements forged into one intense experience. For all of its potential, joy and challenges few of us get any coaching on how to have the most satisfying relationship possible. Some of us got 2 weeks of pre-marital counseling that we hope holds us for the next fifty years! By the way, if you have been married for over twenty years, your relationship will go through at least seven to ten significant changes. Those changes will necessitate that you get "remarried". You will have to rethink together what marriage needs to look like now after that change. Things like, "Ok now that we have a kid how do we do this?" Or, "Now that we have 2 kids how do we do this?" Or "Now that we adopted a kid how do we do this?" Or "Now that we survived that awful cancer scare how do we do this?" Or "now that we have launched our children what do we do now?" Children, health, jobs, locations, family, friends, church, and money all have a significant impact on our marriages. When they change, we change. So, we must adapt. Get remarried in a sense. We often hear, "change is hard". *So why don't we get help?*

Here's what I hear from others (and a few others that I suspect). I list the reason people say they don't get help and then a short response:

- *We hope it will just get better. It worked before, hopefully it will come back round again...right???*
  - o It may. Some studies indicate that a relationship will rebound. However, if you are relearning your attachment or getting "remarried" you will likely find yourself circling back through this hard spot. I tell people that if the same type of struggle appears two times, it's worth talking to someone. You will save yourself a lot of frustration and energy hitting it sooner than later.

- *I feel weird inviting a total stranger into my most vulnerable relationship.*
  - o It is unnerving to be honest. No easy way to start. One of the most significant parts to finding a coach/counselor is they feel safe to you. If you don't feel safe, you won't be honest. If you're not honest, it won't be helpful.

- *If I don't go to a total stranger that means I go to my pastor or another couple I know and then I'm risking that relationship too.*
  - o Getting help involves risking your story. Hopefully, this known source of help will be safe and careful with your story. That means holding confidences, suspending judgements and being gracious to both spouses. That takes a special pastor or couple. Not impossible though. If you have those kinds of relationships, blessed are you-take advantage of them.

- *I don't have time.*
  - o I don't believe you. Just being honest here. This is your most important relationship. If you seriously don't have time, that may be a big part of the problem. Also, one of the biggest factors in letting counseling help you is creating the space. It's not enough to squeeze in a 45-minute appointment. You need to carve out a space to have a weekly communication time and another space to have some fun. I know that sounds like climbing Mount Everest, but it's not.

- *I don't have the money.*
  - o You may not. However, there are possibilities. Your pastor. A marriage class at church. Another mentor couple. A therapist who offers a sliding fee scale. You may not have money, but you have options. Pick one and get started.

- *I don't have the energy.*
  - o Making love is work. It takes time, energy, focus and learning. But what a return on your investment! It makes your time together more enjoyable. It energizes you. Teamwork is enhanced. Learning grows you and your confidence. It's like getting in shape. Not fun when it starts, but it sure feels nice when you get there.

- *I don't have the hope.*
  - o I understand. Often couples feel like they've been working hard and not making progress. That is a clear sign you need some help. If your car breaks down and you don't know what to do...you seek help. If your body is betraying you and you

can't figure it out…you get help. If your computer does weird stuff…you get help. Get help…hope will come.

- *I don't think it will help.*
    - o There's a very good chance you're wrong about that. Some research indicates 9 out of 10 couples report significant improvement after seeing a therapist/counselor. Another more conservative study reported that better than 75% of the couples found it helped. Odds are you too will get help. The sooner you seek help, the better.

One last comment here. I believe getting help works when there are three key factors working together:

1. The therapist/counselor is safe for both of you.
2. The therapist/counselor seems to have skills and knowledge that is helping you find a way through your challenge.
3. You risk being an honest learner. No hiding. No cover-ups.

Made in the USA
Monee, IL
14 January 2021

57656733R00080